Updated
Second Edition

T0372763

Workbook 6
with Online Resources

American English

Caroline Nixon & Michael Tomlinson

Cambridge University Press
www.cambridge.org/elt

Cambridge Assessment English
www.cambridgeenglish.org

www.cambridge.org
Information on this title: www.cambridge.org/ 9781316627228

First published 2009
Second edition 2015
Updated second edition 2017
20 19 18 17 16 15 14 13 12 11 10 9 8 7 6

Printed in Malaysia by Vivar Printing

A catalog record for this publication is available from the British Library

ISBN 978-1-316-62722-8 Workbook with Online Resources 6
ISBN 978-1-316-62756-3 Student's Book 6
ISBN 978-1-316-62705-1 Teacher's Book 6
ISBN 978-1-316-62729-7 Class Audio CDs 6 (4 CDs)
ISBN 978-1-316-62739-6 Teacher's Resource Book with Online Audio 6
ISBN 978-1-316-62793-8 Interactive DVD with Teacher's Booklet 6 (PAL/NTSC)
ISBN 978-1-316-62713-6 Presentation Plus 6
ISBN 978-1-316-63020-4 Posters 6

Additional resources for this publication at www.cambridge.org/elt/kidsboxamericanenglish

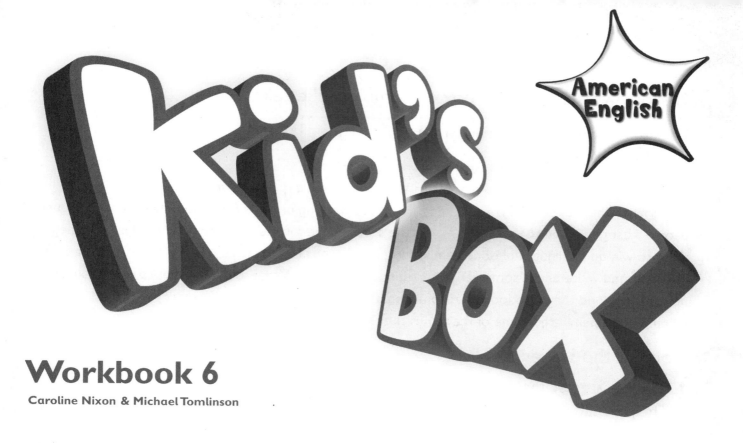

Kid's Box

American English

Workbook 6

Caroline Nixon & Michael Tomlinson

⭐ **High technology**	4
1 Beastly tales	10
Art – Myths and legends	16
2 Tomorrow's world	18
Science – The solar system	24
⭐ **Review 1 and 2**	26
3 The great outdoors	28
Art – Landscape painting	34
4 Food, glorious food!	36
Science – Micro-organisms	42
⭐ **Review 3 and 4**	44
5 Under the ocean	46
Science – Food chains	52
6 Free time	54
Music – Popular music	60

⭐ **Review 5 and 6**	62
7 Dress sense	64
History – Clothes	70
8 Around the world	72
Language – The history of words	78
⭐ **Review 7 and 8**	80
Values 1 & 2 Living with technology	82
Values 3 & 4 Be safe at home	83
Values 5 & 6 Harmony at home	84
Values 7 & 8 Sharing problems	85
Grammar reference	86
Irregular verbs	88
Language Portfolio	89

High technology

1 Choose words from the box to complete the text.

excited	going	~~started~~	thirtieth	math
won	laughed	horrible	year	something

The kids **(1)** _started_ back in school last week, and they're ready for another **(2)** _____ of learning. They're really **(3)** _____ about working on *Kid's Box* again, their ezine for young people. Last year they **(4)** _____ the school prize for the best project, and this year they want to win an international ezine competition if they can. They're **(5)** _____ to visit a lot of places and write about some very interesting things. Last Wednesday they met to talk about their new project, and they also looked at some funny pictures from last year. They **(6)** _____ a lot when they remembered some of the things that happened.

2 Correct the sentences.

1 The kids started their vacations last week. _The kids started back in school last week._
2 They're ready for another month of learning. _____
3 They won the school prize for art. _____
4 They met last Friday. _____
5 They watched some funny DVDs. _____
6 They cried a lot when they remembered. _____

3 Write sentences.

1 _We use a toothbrush to brush our teeth._   4 _____
2 _____   5 _____
3 _____   6 _____

4 Answer the questions.

1 What did you do during your vacation? _____
2 Where did you go? _____
3 Who did you see? _____
4 What did you eat? _____
5 What did you do? _____
6 Who were you with? _____

5 Put the words in groups.

~~math~~	~~friendly~~	~~pizza~~	geography	excited	interested	salt	English
bored	salad	pleased	sandwich	history	pepper	science	

How we feel
friendly

What we eat
pizza

Things we study

MON	math
TUES	
WEDS	
THURS	
FRI	

6 Find the letters on the clock. Make words.

1 It's twenty-five to twelve.   wing
2 It's twenty-five after six.
3 It's twenty to eleven.
4 It's ten after one.
5 It's ten to nine.

7 Write times to make four more words.
You can use the same letters again.

1 It's ten to eleven. (doll)
2
3
4

8 Find and write the adjectives.

iped

ired

uge

errible

mous

orrible

ong

a_mazing_
a
fa
fa
da
da
s
s

h
h
lo
lo
str
str
t
t

~~mazing~~

oft

ngerous

rk

t

ng

potted

ud

wake

9 Unscramble and write the words. Label the pictures.

~~bakydroe~~   shalf irved   cawmeb   corphimneo   adephoshen   toppla

keyboard   ----------------   ----------------   ----------------   ----------------   ----------------

10 Correct the sentences.

1 A laptop is a big heavy computer that we can't carry in a special bag.
A laptop is a small --

2 Speakers are like microphones. We use both of them to see our friends when we chat with them
----

3 The whiteboard is the part of the computer that has the letters and numbers. We use it to draw
----

4 We use a microphone to carry information from one computer to another.
----

11 Which computer should Peter buy? Check (✓) the correct box.

Peter needs a new computer because the one he has is very old. It doesn't have a DVD player, but he isn't unhappy because he doesn't like watching movies on the computer. He has a lot of problems with his old computer when he tries to use the Internet because it is too slow and he can't use it with wifi. The Internet is important for him because he uses it to search for information for his school projects. He also uses his computer a lot to chat with his friends, but he never uses it to play games. He doesn't need to carry his computer when he travels, so he doesn't want a laptop. He thinks it's a good idea to buy a flash drive to ta[k] his projects and songs around to his friend's house.

The KB4
Speakers
DVD player
Big screen - great for playing games
Special keyboard   **$899**

The KB5
Laptop computer
DVD player
Speakers
Better memory
Good for the Internet   **$649**

The KB6
FREE!
DVD player
DVD player
Webcam
Microphone
Speakers
Good for the Internet
Free flash drive   **$749**

12 Write three reasons you chose that computer in your notebook.

13 Connect two words to make one. Write the new word.

1 home ⌐ ball   _____
2 head   board   _____
3 key   room   _____
4 class └─ work   homework_____
5 basket   phones   _____

14 Write another word at the end to make new words.

1 bathroom_____   3 ear_____   5 arm_____   7 white_____
2 book_____   4 hand_____   6 tooth_____   8 snow_____

15 Find eight differences.

In picture a, the boy's chatting online. In picture b, he's watching a movie._____
_____
_____
_____
_____
_____
_____

16 Answer the questions.

1 Can you use a computer? _____
2 Do you write emails? _____
3 Do you use apps to chat with your friends? _____
4 Do you have wifi at home? _____
5 Do you use a flash drive? _____
6 Do you send messages to your friends? _____
7 How do you listen to music? _____
8 Do you prefer headphones or speakers? _____

17 Match the words to make new words.

1	_d_	play	**a**	board	6	_g_	white	**f**	ache
2	__	air	**b**	ball	7	__	business	**g**	board
3	__	key	**c**	store	8	__	head	**h**	ball
4	__	basket	**d**	ground	9	__	super	**i**	man
5	__	book	**e**	port	10	__	volley	**j**	market

18 Listen, check, and say.

Lst wknd ptr wnt 2 hs uncls hs in the cntry. Hs uncl lvs on a frm. Hs a frmr. Ptr hlpd hm wth the anmls. He gt up erly and gt the mlk frm the cws n the egs frm the chckns. Thrs a smll drty lak on the frm n ptr fll in2 it. lol.

When we use text language:
• We take out the vowels:
 clssrm – classroom
• We use words or letters that sound the same, but are shorter:
 hw r u (= How are you?)
• Some people don't use punctuation or capital letters in a short message.

Write it right

19 Write the text above correctly.

Last weekend

20 Write a text message for your friend to read.

21 Read and answer.

1 What time's Diggory giving his talk?

At half past two.

2 What kind of computer does Diggory have?

----

3 What can he use to explain ancient math and technology?

----

4 Who's Sir Doug Bones?

----

5 Why does he want to look under the cloth?

----

6 Who has the calendar at the end?

----

22 Look at the code. Write the secret message.

A	B	C	D	E	F	G	H	I	J	K	L	M

N	O	P	Q	R	S	T	U	V	W	X	Y	Z

T h e   _____

_____

_____

_____ .

? **Do you remember?**

1 10:55 is five to_____ eleven.

2 _____ don't we buy a new computer?

3 I bought a _____ , so now I can see my friends when we talk on the computer.

4 A small computer that we can carry easily is a _____ .

5 _____ and _____ are two new words we can make from "ball," "play," "basket," and "ground."

6 In text language "U" means _____ .

Can do   I can name the parts of a computer.
               I can talk about technology.
               I can write text messages in English.

LOOK again | Going to

We use *going to* to talk about plans.

Affirmative	Negative (n't = not)	Question
I'm (am) going to read.	You **aren't going to** listen to music.	**Is** he **going to** play tennis?
She's (is) going to read.	We **aren't going to** listen to music.	**Are** they **going to** play tennis?
We're (are) going to read.	He **isn't going to** listen to music.	**Am** I **going to** play tennis?

1 Correct the sentences.

1 I're going to be in the play. _I'm going to be in the play._

2 She's going be the lion. _____

3 Do you are going to watch *The Lion King*? _____

4 They isn't going to go to the theater tomorrow. _____

5 What has he going to do on the weekend? _____

6 She hasn't going to wash her hair today. _____

2 Complete the questions. Match them with the answers.

Who	~~Which~~	Where	When	Why	What

1 _Which_ bus are you going to catch?

2 _____ are we going to play soccer?

3 _____ is he going to call?

4 _____ is she going to wash the car?

5 _____ is he going to read?

6 _____ are they going to take the exam?

a He's going to call his mom. ☐

b They're going to take it tomorrow. ☐

c He's going to read his comic book. ☐

d I'm going to catch the number 27. [1]

e In the park. ☐

f Because it's dirty. ☐

3 Look at the code. Write the secret message.

=	H	I	J	K	L	M	N	O	P	Q	R	S	T	U	V	W	X	Y	Z	A	B	C	D	E	F	G
	A	B	C	D	E	F	G	H	I	J	K	L	M	N	O	P	Q	R	S	T	U	V	W	X	Y	Z

AOL   AOLHALY   JSBI   PZ   NVPUN   AV   ZOVD   AOL   WSHF

The _____ ____ __ _____ __ ____ ___ ____

VU   AOL   SHZA   AOBYZKHF   HUK   MYPKHF   VM   QBUL.

__ ___ ____ _____ ___ _____ __ ____.

4 Find six sentences and write them in your notebook.

He isn't	tickets	to rain	animals.
How many	to get	eat	tomorrow.
Are they going	going	do you	monkey.
They didn't	isn't going	for the	an actor.
Lions	choose him	to be	the play?
It	catch and	parts in	want?

5 What are they going to do?

1 Robert's turning on the TV.
He's going to watch TV.

2 Sue's standing outside the castle, and she's holding her camera.

3 The car's very dirty. Mr. White is walking toward it with some water.

4 Some people are standing at the bus stop.

5 The boys are walking to the park. They're carrying a soccer ball.

6 There's some paper in front of Emma, and she's picking up a pen.

6 Think about January next year. Answer the questions.

1 How old are you going to be?
2 What grade are you going to be in?
3 Which subjects are you going to study?
4 Which clubs are you going to join?
5 What are you going to do after school and on which days?
6 Which books are you going to read?
7 Which movies are you going to see?
8 What else are you going to do?

7 Use your answers to write about what you're going to do next year.

In January next year, I'm going to be

8 Find the words. Label the picture.

f	a	i	r	i	e	n
n	e	s	t	o	s	h
a	a	a	u	e	c	o
o	g	g	t	e	a	r
e	l	a	o	h	l	n
f	e	e	o	u	e	f
c	l	a	w	u	s	r

1 _____

2 _____

3 _eagle_ _____

4 _____   **5** _____   **6** _____

9 Look at the other letters in the word search puzzle in Activity 8. Cross out all the vowels that aren't "i." Write the other letters. _____

Which beast is it? _____

10 Look at the picture and correct the sentences.

1 The dragon has fur on its body. _The dragon has scales on its body._ _____

2 The dragon wants to get the parrot's eggs. _____

3 The dragon and the eagle have dangerous hands. _____

4 The dragon has feathers on its wings, but the eagle doesn't. _____

5 The dragon has two ears on its head. _____

6 The eagle's eggs are in a cave. _____

11 Look at these beasts. Invent names and describe them.

1 _This is a "Dinolion."_
It has a dinosaur's
_____
_____
_____

2
_____
_____
_____
_____
_____

3
_____
_____
_____
_____
_____

12 Read and answer "yes" or "no."

The Sphinx existed in ancient Egyptian and ancient Greek mythology. In Greek mythology, the Sphinx had a lion's body, legs, and claws, a snake's tail, an eagle's wings, and a woman's head. The story says that she sat at the door of the ancient city of Thebes to guard it. To go into the city, people had to answer the Sphinx's question. If they got it right, they could go into the city. If they got it wrong, she ate them. The ancient Greek writer Sophocles wrote the question in his work. It was "Which creature goes on four feet in the morning, two feet in the afternoon, and three feet in the evening?" Do you know the answer?

1 The Sphinx was a real animal. no_____
2 She had a bird's wings. _____
3 She had a mammal's tail. _____

4 She stood at the door of Thebes. _____
5 She asked people a question. _____
6 People who didn't know went home. _____

13 Write the words.

1 an ancient story about heroes = myth_____
2 snakes have these on their bodies = _____
3 birds have these on their wings = _____
4 a word for an animal or a creature = _____
5 a very expensive yellow metal = _____
6 some birds make these in trees = _____
7 the home of a king or queen = _____
8 half woman, half fish = _____

14 Now cross out the first letter of each answer in Activity 13. Read the other letters to answer the Sphinx's question.

n	g	a	~~m~~	f	m
c	m	s	b	a	n

__ ___

15 What's going to happen?

The boat is going to break on the rocks. _____ _____

_____ _____ _____

16 Complete the sentences.

| mythical | ~~breathes~~ | math | Thursday | third |
| then | feathers | think | months | clothes |

1 A dragon _breathes_ fire.
2 I'm going to a party, and I want to buy some new _____ to wear.
3 These three children came first, second, and _____ in the race.
4 My father's birthday is on _____ .
5 We had dinner, and _____ we went to the theater.
6 The unicorn is a _____ animal.
7 I _____ we should watch a movie tonight.
8 Parrots are birds with very colorful _____ .
9 There are twelve _____ in a year.
10 Kate's favorite subject is _____ .

17 [20 CD1] Listen, check, and say.

18 Complete the story with "who," "where," or "that."

This is the myth of Icarus, the boy
(1) _who_ flew too close to the Sun
and fell out of the sky. Daedalus,
(2) _____ was Icarus' father, was
a smart artist. Minos, (3) _____
was the King of Crete, asked him to make
a labyrinth (4) _____ was very
difficult to get out of. The labyrinth was
the place (5) _____ a terrible
beast called the Minotaur lived.

Writing longer sentences
Join sentences with **who**, **where**, and **that**.
Sophocles was a writer. He wrote the Sphinx's question in his work.
➔ Sophocles, **who** was a writer, wrote the Sphinx's question in his work.
The nests are made of gold. Griffins live in them.
➔ The nests **where** griffins live are made of gold.
A dragon is a beast. It has scales and big claws.
➔ A dragon is a beast **that** has scales and big claws.

Write it right

19 Now write the rest of the story correctly. Use "who," "where," or "that."

Theseus, / was the son of the king of Athens, decided to save the children from the horrible beast. Ariadne, / was King Minos' daughter, gave Theseus the string / he used when he went into the labyrinth. Theseus went into the place / the beast lived and killed it. The string / Ariadne gave him helped him to find the way out. King Minos wasn't happy. He was very angry with Daedalus because he was the man / gave Ariadne the string. He sent Daedalus to Crete, a small island, / he had to stay with his son, Icarus.

Daedalus made some wings / he used to escape from Crete with his son. Icarus felt very happy and flew too close to the Sun, which burned his wings and feathers. He disappeared into the ocean below. The place / Icarus fell into the ocean is now an island / is called Icaria.

Theseus, who was the son of the King of Athens, decided to save the children from the horrible beast.

20 Read and answer.

1 Where's the Aztec calendar from? <u>A museum in Mexico City.</u>_____
2 Who's lyam Greedy? _____
3 How do you write 6 in the Mayan math system? _____
4 Who was Quetzalcoatl? _____
5 What's in the email? _____
6 Where are Diggory and Emily going to go? _____

21 Complete and match.

1 How am I going to tell the museum in Mexico City? d

2 A spot means one and a _____ means five.

3 It _____ like a phone number to me.

4 I'm a snake, and I have _____ .

5 He was part _____ and part snake.

? **Do you remember?**

1 They aren't going _____ to choose Dan for the part of the monkey.
2 They are going _____ write about exciting beasts.
3 Dragons have _____ on their bodies.
4 Eagles live in _____ in high places.
5 _____ is the day before Friday and the day after Wednesday.
6 The place _____ Icarus fell into the ocean is now an island called Icaria.

Can do
I can talk about what is going to happen.
I can talk about beasts from myths and legends.
I can write a myth.

1 **Choose words from the box to complete the text.**

lot	~~were~~	There	that	whose
was	so	who	many	

Greek myths **(1)** <u>were</u> full of gods and beasts. The 12 most important gods lived on the mountain of Olympus. Each god was important for a different area of life. Zeus was very important because he was the king of the gods and was also the father of **(2)** _____ other gods and heroes. Other important gods were Aphrodite (the goddess of love), Hades (the god of the underworld), Athena (the goddess of the arts), Apollo (the god of music), and Poseidon (the sea god). There were also a **(3)** _____ of different beasts in Greek myths. Some of the famous beasts are Gorgon, a terrible monster who had a snake's head; the Chimera, who had three heads; Hydra, **(4)** _____ head grew again if someone cut it off; Pegasus, a horse that had wings; and the Cerberus, a huge dog with three heads. There were also frightening dragons and sea snakes, **(5)** _____ Greek heroes had a lot of things to worry about!

2 **Read again and answer.**

1 Who was the most important Greek god? <u>Zeus</u>_____
2 Who was Aphrodite? _____
3 Who was the god of music? _____
4 What was special about Gorgon? _____
5 Which beast could fly? _____
6 What's the name of the huge dog with three heads? _____

3 **Write about a legend from your country.**

1 What's the name of the hero/heroes? _____
2 What did he/she do? _____
3 Who did he/she do it with? _____
4 Why is he/she famous? _____

A famous legend from my country is _____
_____
_____

Listen and color and write. There is one example.

2 Tomorrow's world

We use *will* to talk about the future.

Affirmative	Negative (won't = will not)	Question
I'**ll** go to the Moon.	You **won't** travel by car.	**Will** she fly in a rocket?
It'**ll** go to the Moon.	We **won't** travel by car.	**Will** they fly in a rocket?

1 Read and match.

1 We will have
2 She won't go
3 NASA will send a
4 There won't be any
5 Someone will
6 Some people

a invent a carplane.   ☐
b will go to the Moon on vacation.   ☐
c wifi everywhere.   1
d solar satellite next year.   ☐
e to school by bus.   ☐
f cars in a hundred years.   ☐

2 Complete the chart. Check (✓) "Yes" or "No."

Will you ...	Yes	No
1 travel to the Moon?		
2 have the same job as your parents?		
3 have a lot of children?		
4 live in the same town that you live in now?		
5 go to college when you're older?		

3 Now write sentences with "will" or "won't."

I will/won't travel to the Moon.

1 _____
2 _____
3 _____
4 _____
5 _____

4 Read the notes. Complete the sentences.

9:00   Arrive at school. Change clothes for P.E. class.
9:15   Play badminton.
10:00 Take a shower.
10:30 Go to math class.
11:15 Go out to play. Drink some orange juice.

1 When Peter arrives at school, _he'll change his clothes for P.E. class._

2 After he plays badminton, _____ .

3 After he has math, _____ .

4 When he goes out to play, _____ .

5 Will these things happen in 2050? Write sentences with "will" or "won't."

1 Children / classes / home <u>Children won't have classes at home.</u>
2 People / go / Mars _____
3 People / fly / cars _____
4 People / use computers _____
5 Children / have electronic schoolbooks _____
6 People / use more plastic _____

6 Read and complete.

| quickly | ~~shower~~ | won't | arms | cup | will | brush |

This is my new invention to help children in the future. It's a cross between a **(1)** shower and a car wash. It'll have two funny metal **(2)** _____ with big gloves made of rubber. These **(3)** _____ move around and around very **(4)** _____ to wash us with soap and water. One of them will **(5)** _____ our teeth with a toothbrush, too. Outside the shower there'll be a machine to dry us. It'll look like a big **(6)** _____ , and we'll stand under it. We'll take a shower, and we **(7)** _____ have a wet towel.

7 Design and draw an invention to help children in the future.

8 Write about your invention.

9 Label the pictures.

engineer   astronaut   ~~tourist~~   businessman

tourist _____   _____   _____   _____

10 Sort and write the words.

1 Earth_____
2 _____   4 _____
3 _____   5 _____

11 Complete the sentences.

1 Space_____ is the name we give to everything outside Earth's air.

2 An _____ is a person who designs or makes machines or electrical things.

3 We breathe _____ .

4 The planet _____ is where we live.

5 An _____ can travel in space.

6 The _____ goes around our planet. We can see it at night.

7 A _____ visits another town or country on vacation.

8 A man who works in business is called a _____ .

9 A _____ goes very quickly and can take people into space.

12 Read and answer "yes" or "no."

The space race started in 1957 when the Soviet Union sent a satellite into space. It was called Sputnik 1. A satellite is something that goes around Earth. The Soviet Union then sent a dog called Laika into space in Sputnik 2. Next, the U.S.A. sent its own satellite, called Explorer 1, into space. In 1958, the U.S.A. started its space agency, called NASA. Three years later in 1961, Russian Yuri Gagarin became the first person to orbit Earth in a spaceship. It wasn't until July 1969 that the American astronaut Neil Armstrong became the first person to walk on the Moon.

1 The Soviet Union sent the first satellite into space. yes___

2 The first animal in space was a monkey. _____

3 The U.S.A. started NASA in 1959. _____

4 Yuri Gagarin was an astronaut from the U.S.A. _____

5 Gagarin flew around Earth. _____

6 Neil Armstrong was the first man to walk on the Moon. _____

13 Match the ideas about life on Zeron, the space city. Write sentences.

1 telescopes in the windows   **a** to build new houses
2 satellites   **b** to get energy
3 solar panels   **c** to travel into space
4 robots   **d** to look at the stars
5 rockets   **e** to receive signals from space

1

1 <u>We'll have telescopes in the windows to look at the stars.</u>
2 _____
3 _____
4 _____
5 _____

14 Read and answer the riddles.

1 The beginning of Earth, the end of space. The beginning of every end, the end of every place. What am I? <u>"e"</u>

2 What comes once in a minute, twice in a moment, and never in a thousand years?
_____

3 Which letter will come next in this sequence? M, A, M, J, J, A, S, O ... ? _____

4 How will you use the letters in NEW DOOR to make one word? _____

5 Harry was an engineer. His mother had four children. The first was April, the second was May, and the third was June. What was the name of her fourth child? _____

6 A man's looking at a picture of a famous astronaut and he says, "I have no brothers and sisters, but that man's father is my father's son." Who's he looking at? _____

15 Read and complete the circle with names and jobs.

There are three girls and two boys. They're talking about the jobs they think they will (✓) and won't (✗) do in the future.

1 Sarah's sitting between Dave and Mike. The person on Mike's left thinks she'll be an actress, but she won't be a painter.
2 The boy who says he'll be a dentist won't be an actor.
3 The person on Mary's left won't be a photographer, but she thinks she'll be a mechanic.
4 The girl next to Lucy loves cameras, so she'll be a photographer, but she won't be a cook.
5 The boy next to Lucy loves rockets, but he won't be an astronaut. He thinks he'll be a rocket engineer.

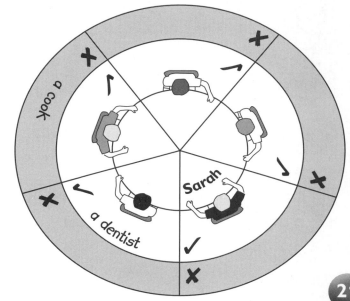

16 Match the rhyming words.

1	c	I'll	a	feel
2	_	she'll	b	knees
3	_	they're	c	smile
4	_	we're	d	here
5	_	he's	e	air

6	g	I'm	f	rule
7	_	who's	g	time
8	_	who'll	h	don't
9	_	won't	i	choose
10	_	let's	j	gets

17 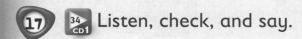 Listen, check, and say.

18 Read the Tourist Space Schedule and answer.

Vacation in Space

Friday, July 17, 2047

7:00   Meet at the Earth Space Station, Houston, Texas, U.S.A.

8:00   Leave Earth in a spaceplane.

8:30   Stop at the Milky Way Star Café for breakfast (hot chocolate and cake pills).

9:30   Put on spacesuits. Get on the KB6 Adventurer space rocket.

12:00 Arrive on the Moon. Walk around and take pictures.

12:30 Go to the Armstrong Moon Restaurant for lunch (chicken salad in an envelope). Take off spacesuits to eat.

1:30   Catch a Moon bus to go to the space port.

2:00   Get on the KB6 Adventurer again. Fly to the Galactica Hotel.

1 How will they leave Earth?
In a spaceplane.

2 Where will they stop for breakfast?

3 What will they have for breakfast?

4 What will they put on?

5 What will they do on the Moon before lunch?

6 Why will they take off their spacesuits?

Connectors
• Remember to use some of these words to join your sentences and sequence them:
When, Then, After that, because, before

Write it right

19 Practice saying your answers with the " 'll" form correctly.

20 Use your answers to write the Space Schedule in your notebook.

The tourists will meet at the Earth Space Station at seven o'clock. Then they'll leave Earth in a spaceplane at eight o'clock. Before they get on the KB6 Adventurer space rocket, they'll stop

21 Read and answer.

1 Why did Iyam Greedy send them tickets to Mexico City?
<u>There are legends about Aztec gold.</u>

2 What did the Aztecs and the Mayas use to measure time? _____

3 When did the Aztec new year start? _____

4 What will be the longest day of the year? _____

5 What's the date now in the story? _____

6 Will they stay in Mexico City tonight? _____

22 Read and order the text. Write the story in your notebook.

technology and their ancient math system. Iyam Greedy, who's a pirate and ☐

notebook and talked about a group of stars. There was a man sitting next to them. He ☐

phone number for Diggory in a letter. When Diggory called the number, Iyam ☐

only wants to get the Aztec gold and be rich, stole the Sun Stone and left a ☐

Diggory Bones is an archeologist who teaches at City College. He had the ☐ 1

On the plane to Mexico City, Diggory and his daughter, Emily, looked at a ☐

man from the plane got into a car with Iyam Greedy and followed their bus. ☐

listened to them talking. When Diggory and Emily caught a bus to Teotihuacan, the ☐

talked about Aztec mythology. Then he sent him two plane tickets in an email. ☐

Sun Stone. This is the name for the Aztec calendar, which he had to talk about Mayan (and Aztec) ☐

? **Do you remember?**

1 In the future there <u>will</u> _____ be spaceplanes.

2 That's not a very good paper plane. It _____ fly very far.

3 _____ are people who fly in space in their job.

4 Our planet is called _____ .

5 In the question "When'll they arrive?" "'ll" is a contraction of _____ .

6 _____ they build a spaceplane for tourists, we'll fly around Earth on our vacation.

Can do
I can talk about what will happen.
I can talk about travel in the future.
I can write about space travel.

23

1 Write the planets in order (1 = closest to the Sun).

| Saturn | Earth | Neptune | ~~Mercury~~ | Jupiter | Venus | Uranus | Mars |

1 <u>Mercury</u>   2 _____   3 _____   4 _____

5 _____   6 _____   7 _____   8 _____

2 Read and complete the fact sheet.

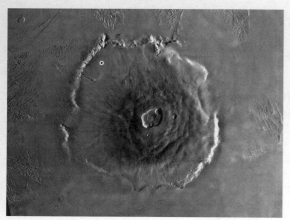

Mars is the fourth planet from the Sun and is often called the red planet. Mars takes 687 days to go around the Sun, so on Mars a year is 687 days long.

Mars has two moons. It also has the biggest volcanic mountain in the solar system. This is called Olympus Mons. It is 27 km high, and it has a diameter of 600 km. There are no rivers or lakes on Mars, so scientists think there is no life there, but they think it's possible that there's water under the ground.

FACT SHEET – PLANETS

Planet: <u>Mars</u>

Position from the Sun: _____

Often called: _____

Orbits the Sun every: _____

How many moons: _____

Interesting facts: _____

----

3 Write about Neptune in your notebook.

FACT SHEET – PLANETS

Planet: Neptune

Position from the Sun: eighth

Often called: big blue planet

Orbits the Sun every: 165 years

How many moons: eight

Interesting facts: • strongest winds (2,000 km/h)

                         • has five rings

                         • coldest planet

Neptune is the eighth planet from the Sun.

4 Look and read. Choose the correct words and write them on the lines.
There is one example.

rockets   a monkey   a theater   stars

You use this to take pictures. It isn't a cell phone.   <u>a camera</u>

~~a camera~~   1   This is a big road where people can drive fast.   ------------------   a lion

2   Astronauts use these to fly into space.   ------------------

3   This is a person who flies a plane.   ------------------

a mouse   4   This day comes after Wednesday.   ------------------   an island

5   This animal is a very big cat. It's called
"the King of the Beasts."   ------------------

6   This is a piece of land in the ocean. There's
water all around it.   ------------------

planets   7   This is the place where you go to see a play.   ------------------   a driver

8   There are a lot of these in the sky. You can
see them clearly at night.   ------------------

gold   9   There are eight of these in our solar system.   ------------------   a stadium

10 This yellow metal is very expensive. People
make rings and bracelets from it.   ------------------

a pilot   Thursday   trees   a highway

Review Units 1 and 2

1 Read the story. Choose a word from the box. Write the correct word next to numbers 1–5.

| tomorrow | engineer | food | will | future | museum | ~~favorite~~ | drive |
| rocket | picture |

Friendly

Friendly is the kids' <u>favorite</u> TV show. It's a comedy, and it's very funny. It's about five friends who all live and study in the same school. Last week the friends had an interview with a special teacher to talk about their **(1)** _____ jobs. They had to think about which school subjects they were good at and where they wanted to work.

Sue wants to study art in college. Jim loves sports and staying in shape and wants to be a firefighter. Peter loves **(2)** _____ , and he says he'll be a cook. Sally says she'll be a cab driver. Jenny's good at English and drama and wants to be an actor. She says that when she's famous, Sally **(3)** _____ drive her to the movie studio, Peter will cook her nice meals, and Sue will paint her a **(4)** _____ and put it in a big important **(5)** _____ . When Jim asks what he'll do for her, Jenny says her house will never catch fire, so he'll have to change his job!

2 Now choose the best name for the story.

Check one box. Past and present ☐   After-school club ☐   Future plans ☐

3 Read and match the jokes.

1 What's green and smells like paint?
2 How does a monster count to 13?
3 Which side of an eagle has the most feathers?
4 What do you get if you cross a blue cat with a red parrot?
5 How many seconds are there in a year?
6 Which animal can jump higher than a house?
7 Where can you find an ocean without water?
8 Why don't mother kangaroos like rainy days?
9 What goes through towns and up and over hills, but doesn't move?
10 What do you get if you cross a parrot with a tiger?

a The outside.
b All of them can. A house can't jump.
c A purple carrot!
d I don't know, but when it talks you should listen carefully!
e Green paint.
f On its fingers!
g A road.
h On a map!
i Twelve: January the second, February the second …
j Because their children have to play inside!

☐
☐
☐
☐
[1]
☐
☐
☐
☐
☐

4 Complete the sentences. Count and write the letters.

1 <u>Space</u> is the place outside Earth's air, where the Moon and planets are. `[5]`

2 A griffin's nest is made of _____ . `[ ]`

3 In text language, "tchnlgy" means _____ . `[ ]`

4 We breathe _____ . It's called "wind" when it moves over Earth. `[ ]`

5 Somebody who works in space is an _____ . `[ ]`

6 Eagles have a lot of _____ on their wings. `[ ]`

7 A small light computer that we can carry easily is a _____ . `[ ]`

8 "What _____ you do?" "I'll ask Michael to help me." `[ ]`

9 The Sun is the only _____ in our solar system. `[ ]`

10 The _____ is the part of the computer that has the letters that we use to write. `[ ]`

11 A space station uses a _____ to send astronauts into space. `[ ]`

12 An _____ designs cars and motorcycles. `[ ]`

13 We use a _____ to see our friends when we're chatting on the Internet. `[ ]`

14 _____ are at the end of a dragon's leg. `[ ]`

5 Write the words in the crossword puzzle. Write the message.

Message boxes: 1 2 3 4 | 5 6 | 7 8 9 10 **s** !

6 Quiz time!

1 What toy animal did Dan have in the audition? <u>He had</u> _____

2 What was the name of Jason's boat? _____

3 Who fought the Minotaur? _____

4 How will tourists fly into space in the future? _____

5 Which planet is the red planet? _____

6 How many moons does Saturn have? _____

7 Write questions for your quiz in your notebook.

27

LOOK again — Past progressive

We use the *past progressive* to describe what was happening in the past.

Affirmative	Negative	Question
I **was climbing** when I fell.	I **wasn't walking.**	**Was** I **playing**?
You **were climbing** when you fell.	He **wasn't walking.**	**Was** she **playing**?
He **was climbing** when he fell.	They **weren't walking.**	**Were** we **playing**?

1 Read and match.

1 She was skating   **a** he saw a tree in front of him. ☐

2 We were cooking sausages   **b** it flew into a tree. ☐

3 You were flying your kite   **c** she fell down. [1]

when

4 He was skiing down the hill fast   **d** the kitchen caught fire. ☐

5 I was sleeping   **e** their train arrived. ☐

6 They were waiting at the station   **f** you called me. ☐

2 Look at the pictures. Answer the questions.

1 Was Betty playing volleyball at a quarter after eleven? <u>Yes, she was.</u>

2 Were Frank and Betty doing their homework at a quarter after five? _____

3 Was Frank playing the guitar at ten after seven? _____

4 Were Frank and Betty having lunch at twenty-five after one? _____

5 Was Betty brushing her teeth at half past eight? _____

6 Were Frank and Betty watching TV at ten to five? _____

3 Write four more questions about Frank and Betty in your notebook.

4 Correct two mistakes in each sentence.

1 Richard was ~~run~~ for the bus when he ~~dropping~~ his bag. <u>running, dropped</u>

2 Peter and Fred was playing baseball when it start to rain. _____

3 I were putting the food on the table when the man call. _____

4 Vicky was sail in the ocean when she hitted a rock. _____

5 Match the sentences with the pictures.

1 We looked at our map. We had to walk through a forest to get to the campsite.

2 In this picture we were eating the sandwiches that John and David got from the café. We couldn't eat the sausages because they burned black!

3 Last week I went camping with my friends John and David. When we got off the bus, it was raining.

4 Our feet were hurting after the long walk, and we were tired and hungry when we arrived.

5 It was getting late when we were walking through the forest, and it was very dark.

6 This is a picture of me when I was cooking the sausages. I'm not a very good cook.

6 Read and answer "yes" or "no."

1 He went camping with his friends David and John. _yes_

2 It was raining when they got off the bus. _____

3 They had to walk up a hill to get to the campsite. _____

4 The Sun was coming up when they were walking through the forest. _____

5 Their feet were hurting when they arrived at the campsite. _____

6 When he was cooking the sausages, he burned them. _____

7 Read and answer.

Hi Sarah,

This is a funny picture of me at the airport! We were waiting for our plane when I started to feel hungry, so I decided to buy some ice cream. There weren't many people waiting to buy one. When I was giving the man the money, someone put a suitcase down on the floor behind me. I didn't see it! I was starting to eat my ice cream when my mom called me to go and catch my plane. I turned quickly, and I fell over the suitcase … and my face went into my ice cream! When I stood up, I had chocolate ice cream on my nose! My mom thought I looked really funny, so she took the picture!

How was your vacation?

See you soon,

Katy

1 What were Katy and her mom doing at the airport? _They were waiting for the plane._

2 Were there many people waiting to buy ice cream? _____

3 When did someone put a suitcase down behind her? _____

4 What was she starting to do when her mom called her? _____

5 What did her mom think when she stood up? _____

8 Look at the picture. Find the words a–l in the word search puzzle.

s	o	o	p	d	r	o	h	r	y	r
l	e	r	f	n	c	w	e	s	t	f
e	b	c	e	o	n	t	k	t	g	l
e	a	h	e	s	r	n	o	s	h	a
p	c	s	n	k	t	e	n	t	i	s
i	t	a	t	a	z	y	s	a	l	h
n	o	e	m	p	n	r	e	t	l	l
g	r	e	x	p	l	o	r	e	r	i
b	c	s	q	i	u	g	r	l	a	g
a	h	t	n	x	s	o	u	t	h	h
g	b	a	c	k	p	a	c	k	h	t

9 Write the words. Add the correct letters from Activity 8.

1 camp_____ = to live and sleep outdoors   [a]

2 _____ = a bag you can sleep in   [ ]

3 _____ = the opposite of north   [ ]

4 _____ = something you can use to see when it's dark   [ ]

5 _____ = a high place that's lower than a mountain   [ ]

6 _____ = a place where you can sleep   [ ]

10 Write definitions for three more words in Activity 8. Add the correct letters.

_____ [ ]

_____ [ ]

_____ [ ]

11 Look at the code. Write the secret message in your notebook.

> N = north   S = south   E = east   W = west

When – 5E – 4N – 2W – 3S – 2W – 1N – 3E – 2S – 4N – 2W – 3S – 2W – 2N – 5E – 1S – 2W – 2S – 2W – 1E – 2N – 2W – 2N – 1E – 1S – 2E – 1W – 2E – 2S – 1E.

a	warm,	carry	walking	always	are
You	dry	and	jacket	a	should
fruit,	hills,	some	a	you	take
backpack.	the	a	in	cell	phone.
When	of	water,	bottle	should	you

12 Read the sentences. Draw and write on the map.

 The New Forest is 5 km north of Starton.

 The hills are 3 km east of the New Forest.

 There's a bridge over the river 5 km west of the New Forest.

2 km south of the hills there's a hotel. Its name is the Happy Inn.

There's a lake 5 km west of Starton. It's called Windymere.

Old Hampton is 2 km north of Windymere.

 The campsite is 3 km east of Old Hampton.

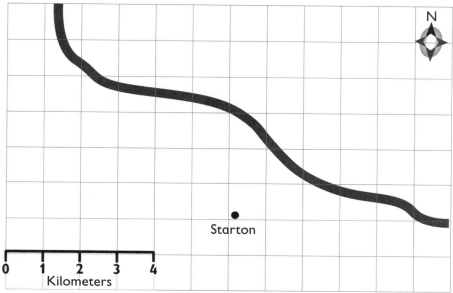

13 Now draw these things on the map in Activity 12. Write the directions.

The flashlight is _____.

The backpack is _____.

The umbrella is _____.

The suitcase is _____.

14 Find the letters on the clock. Write the words.

1 It's a quarter to eight. <u>south</u>_____

2 It's five after ten. _____

3 It's twenty-five after eight. _____

4 It's a quarter after six. _____

5 It's twenty after ten. _____

15 Write times to make four more words in your notebook.

Circle the correct word.

1 It's cold. I need to put on my **coat** / **goat**.

2 The explorers found a **cave** / **gave** in the mountains.

3 She kicked the soccer **call** / **ball** across the field.

4 Kate and John **came** / **game** to the soccer game.

5 Our teacher said the plate was made of **class** / **glass**.

6 The actor let me **hold** / **gold** the award he won.

7 He was swimming at the beach when it **got** / **hot** windy.

8 She won a **cold** / **gold** medal at the Olympic Games.

  Listen, check, and say.

 Read and complete.

a weekend	Friday	June 14
family	tent for five	~~website~~

12 Greenfield Road

Kidsbridge

U.S.A.

March 20

Sunnyday Campgrounds

Cornfield Lane

Hillside

Dear Sir or Madam,

I saw your (1) __website____ on the Internet, and I'm writing to get some information about your campgrounds.

I'd like to come with my (2) _____, and we'd like to stay for (3) _____, from (4) _____, June 12, to Sunday (5) _____. Could you please tell me if you have a space for these dates?

We don't have a tent, so I would also like more information about renting a (6) _____. Could you please tell me how much this will cost?

On your website it says there's a swimming pool close to the campgrounds. Could you please send me the pool's schedule?

Sincerely,

Michael Wishful

 Write a letter to the campgrounds. Use the information below.

You want to go with your seven friends for a week in August. You want to go from Tuesday through Monday. You'd like information about horseback riding. There's a riding school at the campgrounds.

Write it right

Asking for information
- I'm writing to get some information about ...
- I would like to know ...
- Could you please tell me if/when/what/how ... ?
- Could you please give/send me ... ?

Dear Sir or Madam,

I saw your _____

_____

_____

_____

_____

_____

_____

_____

20 Read and answer.

1 Who was getting out of the car behind them? <u>Richard Tricker</u>

2 Where's the Temple of Quetzalcoatl? _____

3 How far is Mexico City from the hotel? _____

4 Why does the man know about this place? _____

5 What does the long street join? _____

6 Was Diggory expecting to see Iyam there? _____

21 Put the verbs into the past.

The story of Mexico City

Around 1325, some young Aztec men **(1)** <u>were getting</u> (are getting) food for their people when they **(2)** _____ (see) an eagle. It **(3)** _____ (is sitting) on a plant that **(4)** _____ (is growing) on a rock in the middle of a lake called Texcoco. They **(5)** _____ (think) it **(6)** _____ (is) a special sign, and they **(7)** _____ (decide) to build their city there.

The Aztecs **(8)** _____ (are) great engineers. They **(9)** _____ (take) the water away from the lake to make the island bigger. They **(10)** _____ (build) canals so people **(11)** _____ (can) move around the city by boat, and bridges that they **(12)** _____ (take) away at night to protect their city. They **(13)** _____ (call) their city Tenochtitlan, and it **(14)** _____ (becomes) one of the biggest and most important cities in the world at that time. The Aztecs **(15)** _____ (are) very rich because they **(16)** _____ (have) land, farms, markets, and stores. They **(17)** _____ (use) the Mayan number system and calendar and they **(18)** _____ (study) the stars and the night sky carefully. Like the ancient Egyptians, they **(19)** _____ (write) with pictures on a kind of paper. The name of the Aztec people at the time **(20)** _____ (is) "the Mexica."

Do you remember?

1 What <u>were</u> you doing at six o'clock yesterday?

2 I was _____ TV.

3 When I go camping, I sleep in a _____ in my tent.

4 Marco Polo traveled _____ from China to Italy.

5 The teacher told the _____ to do their homework.

6 _____ you please send me a schedule?

Can do I can use the past progressive tense to talk about the past.

I can talk about the country and follow directions.

I can write a letter asking for information.

33

1 **Read and choose the right words.**

1 In ancient paintings, the
  country wasn't ...   **a** colorful.   **b** there.   **c** (important.)

2 Landscape painting became
  popular in the ...   **a** 5th century.   **b** 18th century.   **c** 20th century.

3 Artists were trying to copy ...   **a** nature.   **b** other artists.   **c** exams.

4 The French impressionists
  started in the ...   **a** 1850s.   **b** 1860s.   **c** 1870s.

5 The impressionists used ...   **a** big brush strokes.   **b** thick lines.   **c** small spots.

6 Gauguin and Van Gogh used ...   **a** black and white.   **b** bright colors.   **c** dark colors.

2 **Read and draw a picture. Then compare with your friend.**

This picture is a landscape on a sunny day. The top quarter of the picture is the sky that has a big bright sun in the top left-hand corner. On the other side of the page there are three high mountains that have a little snow on top.

There is a stream that comes down from the mountain in the middle and ends in a lake in the bottom right-hand corner of the picture.

There are five tents at a campsite that is to the right of the river. The tents are all different colors and sizes.

On the left of the picture we can see a small hotel. There are some gardens around the hotel, and on one side of the hotel there's a parking lot. There are two cars in the parking lot.

3 **Write about one of the pictures from Student's Book page 35 in your notebook.**

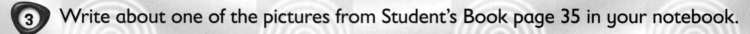

  This picture is a landscape on

Listen and write. There is one example.

The vacation camp

	Name of camp:	Lake Camp
1	Price:	.... dollars a night
2	When:	.... through October 10th
3	Name of lake:	....
4	Take:	....
5	Camp phone number:	....

4 Food, glorious food!

LOOK again   Count and non-count nouns

Count nouns	Non-count nouns
We can count them: strawberries, olives …	We can't count them: water, bread …
There **aren't enough** chairs.	There **isn't enough** water.
There **are too many** people.	There**'s too much** bread.

1 Follow the non-count food words.

How much? →

breakfast	water melon	strawberry	chips	egg	fries	lunch	lime
orange	burger	fruit juice	chocolate	lemonade	soup	lemon	orange juice
bread	carrot	flour	sandwich	mango	pasta	sausage	water
rice	milk	meat	coconut	grape	tea	pea	pepper
vegetable	picnic	olives	dinner	beans	coffee	sugar	salt

→ Only a little.

2 Read and match.

1 In some countries there isn't   **a** because she felt sick.

2 They couldn't make any bread   **b** enough food for everyone to eat.

3 He didn't have many eggs,   **c** because they didn't have enough flour.

4 We didn't feel well   **d** so they decided to give some to their friends.

5 They had too many strawberries,   **e** so he bought some more at the supermarket.

6 She didn't eat much at lunchtime   **f** because we ate too much ice cream at the party.

   □ | 1 | □ □ □ □

3 Read and choose the right words.

1 I feel sick because I ate **too many** / (**too much**) chocolate this morning.

2 I can't buy that because I don't have **enough** / **too many** money.

3 Are there **too many** / **too much** sandwiches?

4 There aren't **enough** / **too much** buses in my town.

5 I like going to the beach when there aren't **too much** / **too many** people.

6 There isn't **enough** / **too much** juice for everyone.

4 Write four sentences in your notebook about your city.

There are too many cars.
There aren't enough parks.

5 Complete the sentences.

| too many | enough | is |
| too much | don't have | enough |

1 There aren't __enough__ sandwiches for us.
2 There are _____ people on this bus.
3 Do you have _____ time to help me with the cake, Peter?
4 Oh, no! I _____ enough money!
5 There _____ enough milk for everyone.
6 I think we have _____ homework this weekend.

6 Complete the conversation. Write a letter (A–F) for each answer.

A OK. We won't have sausages. I know. Let's have some rice and chicken.
B Let me see … No, I'm sorry. We don't have enough spaghetti.
C That's a good idea. So it's chicken, rice, and a salad.
D Yes, we all like pizza, but there isn't enough flour or enough cheese.
E I don't know. What would you like?
F How about some sausages and a salad?

1 What are we going to have for lunch, Dad? **E**
2 Can we have spaghetti, please? It's my favorite. ☐
3 What about pizza then? Can you make us a pizza, please? ☐
4 OK, Dad, what ideas do you have? ☐
5 Um, no thanks. I've had too many sausages this week. I had some yesterday and on Monday. ☐
6 That sounds better. Can we have a salad, too, please? ☐
Great. Let's start cooking.

7 Write about the picture. Use "too much," "too many," "enough," and the words in the box.

| chair | fork | water | pasta |
| cake | banana | plate | |

There are enough chairs. _____
_____
_____
_____
_____
_____
_____

8 What do you think? Answer the questions.

1 Do you eat enough fruit?
_____
2 Do you eat enough fish?
_____
3 Do you eat too much sugar?
_____
4 Do you eat too much candy?
_____
5 Do you eat too many fries?
_____
6 Do you drink enough water?
_____

9 Label the pictures.

| butter | cookie | chopsticks | jelly | ~~snack~~ | pan | sauce | popcorn |

1 snack

2 _____

3 _____

4 _____

5 _____

6 _____

7 _____

8 _____

10 Write the words.

1 We put this on food to make it taste better. It can be hot or cold. sauce

2 This is something we eat between meals. _____

3 These pieces of wood or plastic are used for eating. _____

4 This is made from fruit. We can put it on bread. _____

5 We use this to cook in. _____

6 A lot of children like these snacks. They are usually round. _____

7 This snack is popular when people go to the movies. _____

8 You can put this on the bread first when you make sandwiches. _____

11 Write definitions for these words.

1 sandwich _____
_____

2 strawberry _____
_____

3 knife _____
_____

12 Read and complete the sentences with 1, 2, 3, or 4 words.

Potato chips are very popular as a snack all over the world. George Crum invented them in the U.S.A. At the restaurant where he worked, fries were popular. One day someone wasn't happy because the fries were too thick. Crum made them thinner and thinner until finally, he made fries that were too thin to eat with a fork. The man in the restaurant was happy and people around the world started to eat potato chips. In Britain, fries are called "chips" and potato chips are called "crisps."

1 Potato chips are a very popular snack all over the world.

2 A man from _____ invented them.

3 He made the first potato chips because a man thought his fries _____.

4 Finally, Crum made fries that were _____ with a fork.

5 Potato chips are called "crisps" in _____.

13 Match the children with their snacks.
Write sentences.

Helen   Katy   Michael

Sarah   David   Robert

1 Helen's favorite snack is bread and butter.
2 _____
3 _____
4 _____
5 _____
6 _____

14 Read the poem. Find the word.

The first letter in 'snack'. I'm hungry, you see. | s |

The second in "mango." The fruit's from a tree. | |

The third in "sausage." A hot dog to eat. | |

The fourth in "popcorn." Salty or sweet. | |

The fifth in "butter." I love it on bread. | |

It's something to do with food, I said.

Look at the word and write the letter.

With me, for sure, a dish will taste better.

What am I? _____

15 Read and answer "yes"
or "no."

Chopsticks

People in Asia use
many different
things to eat
with, for example,
hands, spoons,
forks, knives, and
chopsticks.

Chopsticks can
be big or small. Most Chinese chopsticks are
about 25 cm long. For cooking, they also use
longer chopsticks, which can be more than
50 cm long. In Japan, chopsticks are shorter,
and they come to a point at one end.

Chopsticks are made of a number of
materials, but most are made of wood or
plastic. A long time ago they put silver on the
end of the chopsticks.

**Things you should and shouldn't do
when you eat with chopsticks**

- Do not move your chopsticks around.
- Do not pick food up by making a hole
  in it with your chopsticks.
- Do not pull dishes toward you with
  chopsticks. Use your hands.
- Pull dishes close to you when eating.
  Put them back after you use them.
- You can lift your dish up to your mouth to
  eat small pieces of food.

1 Chopsticks are always long. no ____
2 They are the same size in Japan
  and China. _____
3 They are usually made of plastic
  or wood. _____
4 Use them to make holes. _____
5 Move your chopsticks a lot. _____
6 Pick your bowl up. _____

16 Match the rhyming words

1	c	enough	a	water
2	_	straight	b	half
3	_	daughter	c	puff
4	_	laugh	d	flights
5	_	lights	e	eight

6	h	cough	f	caught
7	_	through	g	right
8	_	thought	h	off
9	_	high	i	zoo
10	_	night	j	why

17 [23 CD2] Listen, check, and say.

18 Read and order the instructions.

Bread and tomato snack

Ingredients:
- ❖ 8 slices of bread
- ❖ 3 large tomatoes
- ❖ Olive oil
- ❖ 1 small onion
- ❖ 1 piece of garlic
- ❖ Black pepper

What you do:

[ ] Cover each side of the bread with oil. Take the skin off the garlic and cut it in half.

[ ] Then chop the onion into very small pieces. Mix with the tomatoes and a little pepper.

[ ] Rub the garlic over both sides of the bread. Place on a metal tray and cook for 15 minutes.

[ ] After 15 minutes, take the bread out of the oven. Put some tomato mixture onto each piece of bread. Put it back in the oven for another 5 minutes.

[1] Turn the oven on at 200°C.

[ ] While that's cooking, take the skin off the tomatoes and then chop them.

A recipe
- A recipe gives instructions so someone can cook something.
- First we include all the food we need. These are the **ingredients**.
- Then we give careful, numbered **instructions** about how to cook the food.

Write it right

19 Look at the ingredients and the pictures. Write the recipe. Use these words.

~~break~~	heat	mix
cut	put	

Cold chocolate cookie cake

1 Break the cookies into small pieces.

Ingredients:

75 g   25 g   1 tbsp   175 g   200 g

Instructions:

1    2    3

4    5    6

20 Read and answer.

1 Why will Diggory have to work quickly? <u>They have only enough food for three days.</u>
2 When will Iyam tell Diggory where the Sun Stone is? _____
3 Where are the secret caves? _____
4 Why was corn important to the Mayas and the Aztecs? _____
5 What did the Aztecs eat with chocolate? _____
6 What else did the Aztecs eat? _____

21 Correct the sentences.

1 Emily didn't ask Iyam enough questions.
<u>Emily asked Iyam too many questions.</u>

2 There are pictures of sushi on the Sun Stone.
_____

3 Butter was the most important Aztec food.
_____

4 The door to the caves is about three kilometers west.
_____

5 Iyam shouldn't run because the ground is moving.
_____

6 Diggory asked Emily to get him some chopsticks.
_____

? **Do you remember?**

1 We have too <u>many</u> strawberries.
2 We don't have _____ milk.
3 I love butter and apple _____ on my bread in the morning.
4 People in China often use _____ to eat with.
5 _____ rhymes with "half."
6 After you mix the tomatoes, _____ the mixture on the bread.

Can do   I can use count and non-count nouns.
I can talk about food.
I can write a recipe.

1 Match the words with the definitions.

1 y e a s t
2 f r i d g e
3 m i c r o - o r g a n i s m
4 b a c t e r i a
5 y o g u r t

a a place where we keep our food cold ☐
b something we put in bread to make the mixture grow 1
c this is made of milk mixed with bacteria ☐
d a very small living thing ☐
e this can be good or bad and can grow on food ☐

2 Now look at the letters in the gray boxes in Activity 1. Find a food word.

----

3 Read and match.

1 Keep hot food hot
2 Keep cold food cold
3 Wash fruit and vegetables carefully before you eat or cook them
4 Don't cook with pets in the kitchen
5 Keep meat on the bottom shelf of the fridge

because

a animals can carry bacteria. ☐
b bacteria grow above 5°C. ☐
c bacteria grow below 70°C. 1
d it is colder, and meat juices cannot fall onto other food. ☐
e they grow outside where there can be a lot of bacteria. ☐

4 Read about an English cheese. Then write about your favorite food from your region.

Stilton cheese is sometimes called the king of English cheeses. It is famous for its strong smell and blue veins. Stilton is made from cow's milk. Only three places in England can make real Stilton cheese: Derbyshire, Nottinghamshire, and Leicestershire. It takes about nine weeks to make Stilton, and some people keep it for a few more weeks before they eat it. This is because they like the cheese to be softer and even smellier!

My favorite food from my region is ...

5 Look at the three pictures. Write about this story. Write 20 or more words.

....

....

....

....

Review Units 3 and 4

1 Read the story. Choose a word from the box. Write the correct word next to numbers 1–5.

| flashlight | backpack | was | too | camp | map | tents | ~~country~~ | were | enough |

Friendly

Last week's episode of *Friendly* was really funny because there was a field trip to the country_____. The teachers were taking their students to a forest to **(1)** _____ . On Friday afternoon when they were waiting for the bus outside the school, Jenny arrived with a really big heavy suitcase. She said that her **(2)** _____ wasn't very big, and she had a lot of equipment.

On the way to the campsite, Sally sat next to the bus driver because she wanted to watch her drive, look at the directions, and follow them on her **(3)** _____ .

When they got to the forest, all five of them had to help Jenny pull her suitcase across the field to the **(4)** _____ . The ground was too soft, and it was really hard work. When they were pulling the suitcase, it fell over again and again.

It was dinnertime when they arrived at the campsite, and they were dirty, tired, and hungry. Jenny wasn't very happy when she discovered she couldn't use her hairdryer. She was surprised because she couldn't connect it to any electricity in the wall of the tent! Peter was really unhappy because he wanted to cook sausages and beans, but Jim thought a fire was **(5)** _____ dangerous in a forest. Jim took some peanut butter and jelly sandwiches out of his backpack, Sally said she had some popcorn and cookies, and they all laughed when Sue said she was carrying enough cold sushi and chopsticks for everyone! They all agreed that they were eating the strangest camping menu ever!

2 Now choose the best name for the story.

Check one box.   A drive in the country ☐   Jenny's big suitcase ☐   Forest fire ☐

3 Which is the one that doesn't belong and why?

1 soup   butter   jelly   (cookie)
It's a count noun._____

2 chopsticks   fork   flashlight   spoon
_____

3 best   north   east   south
_____

4 sandwich   sauce   pan   snack
_____

5 tent   cave   sleeping bag   backpack
_____

6 pasta   bread   cake   cheese
_____

44

4 Complete the sentences. Count and write the letters.

1 The opposite of east is
   _west_____.

   `4`

2 They traveled from Italy to China. It was a long _____ .

   ☐

3 A _____ is like a small house. We sleep in it when we camp.

   ☐

4 A _____ is higher than a hill.

   ☐

5 They use _____ to eat sushi in Japan.

   ☐

6 We use a _____ to see in the dark when we go camping.

   ☐

7 I don't like this soup. There's _____ much salt in it.

   ☐

8 Go from one place to another. _____

   ☐

9 How _____ butter do we need?

   ☐

10 A bag that we carry on our back is a _____ .

   ☐

11 There were too _____ people at the beach.

   ☐

12 "What _____ he doing when he fell?" "He was skiing."

   ☐

13 Something light that we eat between meals when we're hungry is a _____ .

   ☐

14 We only had 50 g of flour. We didn't have _____ flour to make cookies.

   ☐

5 Write the words in the crossword puzzle. Write the message.

| | w | e | s | ¹⁰t |

| 1 | 2 | 3 | 4 | 5 | 6 | 7 | | 8 | 9 | 10 |

| | | | | | | | | | | t |

6 Quiz time!

1 When did Alex break his arm?
  When he was _____

2 How did impressionist artists paint?
  _____

3 Name an impressionist artist.
  _____

4 Why couldn't the kids make the cake?
  _____

5 Name two kinds of micro-organisms.
  _____

6 How do we make yogurt?
  _____

7 Write questions for your quiz in your notebook.

45

LOOK again | Present perfect and adverbs

We **still** haven't chosen a project. (= But we have to do it soon.)

The rescue people have been here **since** ten o'clock.
(= When? A point in time: time, date, day, etc.)

It's been here **for** about three hours.
(= How long? How many minutes, hours, days, weeks, etc.)

1 Read and choose the right words.

1 Mr. Schwarz has taught me German (for) / since / still three years.

2 It hasn't snowed since **three days / Saturday / two weeks**.

3 I **still / for / since** haven't finished this activity.

4 They **are / have / were** worked here for a year.

5 She hasn't caught a fish **for / since / still** two hours.

2 Complete the sentences with "for" or "since."

1 She's lived in her town _since_ 2008.

2 My little brother has studied English _____ six months.

3 I haven't seen Peter _____ Monday.

4 Mom has had her favorite jacket _____ ten years!

5 I haven't eaten anything _____ nine o'clock.

3 Look at the code (a = _____). Write the secret message.

a	b	c		j	k	l		s	t	u
d	e	f		m	n	o		v	w	x
g	h	i		p	q	r		y	z	

I've _____ _____

_____, _____

, _____

.

.

4 Write a message in code in your notebook.

5 Find and write four sentences.

liked fishing	three o'clock.	this class since
in that apartment for	five years.	We've been in
~~He's loved~~	I've	for nine months.
started school.	They've lived	~~math since he~~

He's loved math since he _____

_____

_____

_____

6 Write sentences about you with "for" or "since."

1 (this room)   I've been in this room for ten minutes. _____

2 (this class)   _____

3 (best friend) _____

4 (this school) _____

5 (my house)   _____

6 (English)   _____

7 Use the ideas in Activity 6 to write questions to ask your friend.

1 How long have you been in this room? _____

2 _____

3 _____

4 _____

5 _____

6 _____

8 Read and complete the chart.

It's 12 o'clock. There are four children on a bus. Peter was the first boy on the bus. He's been on the bus for ten minutes now, but he's going to get off at the next stop, in two minutes.

David was the last to get on. He got on two minutes ago, but he's going to get off last.

Helen has been on the bus for four minutes. She's going to get off at the same stop as Emma.

Emma has been on the bus for the same time as Helen. She's going to get off at the stop after Peter, in four minutes.

Helen and Emma are going to get off the bus seven minutes before David.

	Got on the bus?	Going to get off the bus?	How long on the bus in total?
Peter	11:50		
David			
Helen			
Emma			

9 Complete the crossword puzzle.

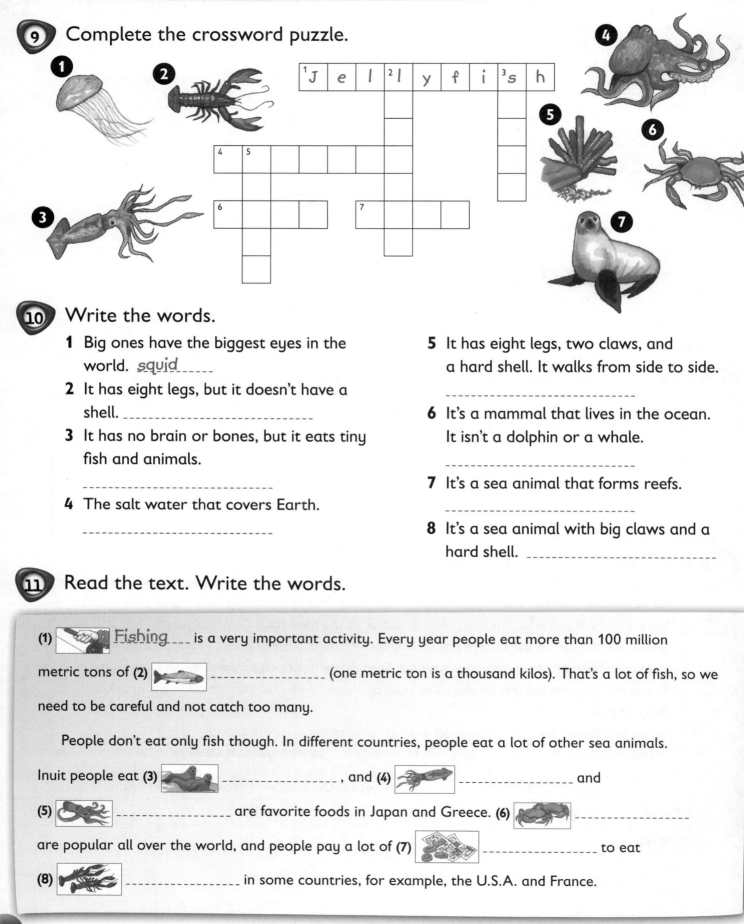

1 ... **2** ...

^{1}J e l ^{2}l y f i ^{3}s h

4 **5** ...

6 ... **7** ...

3 ...

4 **5** **6** **7**

10 Write the words.

1 Big ones have the biggest eyes in the world. <u>squid</u>

2 It has eight legs, but it doesn't have a shell. _____

3 It has no brain or bones, but it eats tiny fish and animals.

_____

4 The salt water that covers Earth.

_____

5 It has eight legs, two claws, and a hard shell. It walks from side to side.

_____

6 It's a mammal that lives in the ocean. It isn't a dolphin or a whale.

_____

7 It's a sea animal that forms reefs.

_____

8 It's a sea animal with big claws and a hard shell. _____

11 Read the text. Write the words.

(1) <u>Fishing</u> ____ is a very important activity. Every year people eat more than 100 million

metric tons of **(2)** _____ (one metric ton is a thousand kilos). That's a lot of fish, so we

need to be careful and not catch too many.

People don't eat only fish though. In different countries, people eat a lot of other sea animals.

Inuit people eat **(3)** _____ , and **(4)** _____ and

(5) _____ are favorite foods in Japan and Greece. **(6)** _____

are popular all over the world, and people pay a lot of **(7)** _____ to eat

(8) _____ in some countries, for example, the U.S.A. and France.

12 Circle twelve words. Which two are different? Why?

beautiful loud angeroustrongreaturtlexcitedolphinicexcitinggoodirty

_____ and _____ are different. They are _____ .

13 Compare these sea animals. Use adjectives from Activity 12 and your own ideas.

1 jellyfish – seals   _Jellyfish are more dangerous than seals._____
2 coral – an octopus   _____
3 an octopus – a jellyfish _____
4 turtles – lobsters   _____
5 a whale – a squid   _____
6 a shark – a crab   _____

14 Read, color, and write.

Find the octopus that is sitting on the big rock. Color it purple. Next, look for the squid. There are three. Color the smallest squid yellow. At the bottom of the picture there's a lot of coral. Color the coral red. Have you found the lobster? It's in the bottom left corner of the picture. Write "lobster" above it. At the top of the picture there are some jellyfish. Color the biggest one blue. There's only one more animal to color. It's the crab. There are three crabs, but color only the crab that is inside the big shell. Color it pink.

15 Read and match.

1 The world's first coral reef   a is the Great Barrier Reef in Australia.
2 Storms can   b appeared about 500 million years ago.   [1]
3 Scientists have used coral reefs c they make beautiful white sand.
4 When parrot fish eat coral,   d to make a lot of different medicines.
5 The biggest reef in the world   e break coral reefs.

16 Write the words in the columns.

~~waited~~   invited   waterfall   enough   understand
astronaut   magazine   eaten   between   important
about   octopus   coral   explorer   engineer

1 ••	**2** ••	**3** •••	**4** •••	**5** •••
waited				

17 Listen, check, and say.

18 Read and complete the fact sheet.

Seahorses are one of the ocean's most interesting animals. They are small fish, but their head looks like a horse.

They are different from most other fish because they don't have scales. They have thin skin over the top of bones. There are more than 32 kinds of seahorses, and they are different sizes and live in different parts of the world. They can live in coral reefs or in water that is not very deep. They swim slowly and can change their color so that other fish don't eat them. Seahorses eat small fish and krill.

The biggest seahorses can be up to 30 cm long, and the smallest is no longer than 3 cm from head to tail.

I think they are the most beautiful sea animal.

Write it right

A report
• When you write a report, you first need to organize the information.
• Make a fact sheet with your information. Include interesting facts.
• Give your report a structure: Introduction – Body – Conclusion

FACT SHEET – SEAHORSES

Body: small, head like
                 a horse

Different kinds: _____

Where: _____

How it moves: _____

Food: _____

Interesting fact: _____

_____

19 Make a sea animal fact sheet in your notebook. Write a report.

20 Read and answer.

1 What has Emily found? <u>She has found a flashlight.</u>

2 What did Quetzalcoatl get at Teotihuacan? _____

3 What kind of shell has Diggory seen? _____

4 Why is Iyam like this animal? _____

5 Was gold a treasure for the Aztecs? _____

6 What is Richard going to do if they don't help Iyam? _____

21 Write sentences from the story.

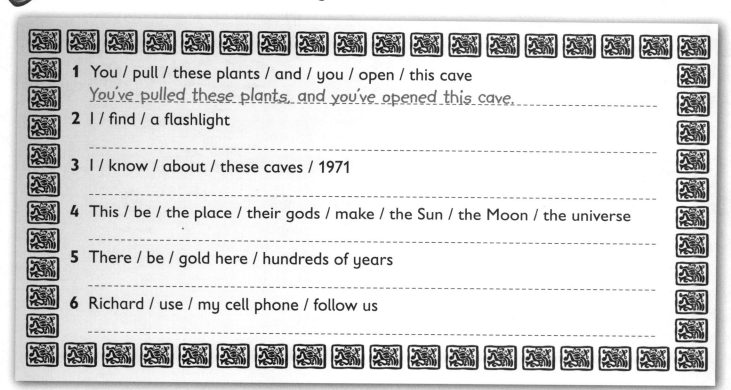

1 You / pull / these plants / and / you / open / this cave
<u>You've pulled these plants, and you've opened this cave.</u>

2 I / find / a flashlight
_____

3 I / know / about / these caves / 1971
_____

4 This / be / the place / their gods / make / the Sun / the Moon / the universe
_____

5 There / be / gold here / hundreds of years
_____

6 Richard / use / my cell phone / follow us
_____

? **Do you remember?**

1 I've been here <u>since</u> _____ seven o'clock.

2 She's lived in this town _____ five years.

3 The Pacific _____ is the biggest in the world.

4 I think _____ reefs are really beautiful.

5 "Engineer" has _____ syllables, and the stress is at the _____ of the word.

6 Seahorses can change _____ .

Can do

I can talk about things that have happened using *for* and *since*.   ☹ 😐 🙂

I can talk about sea animals.   ☹ 😐 🙂

I can write a report about sea animals.   ☹ 😐 🙂

1 Read and label the pictures.

In the Arctic the biggest land animal, and the top predator on land, is the polar bear. Polar bears' favorite food is seals, but they sometimes eat small beluga whales if the whales can't move in the Arctic ice. There are many different kinds of seals in the Arctic, and they eat a lot of sea animals. The most important food for seals is fish. Most of the fish eat zooplankton, and the zooplankton live by eating phytoplankton.

| seal   zooplankton   ~~phytoplankton~~   polar bear   fish |

 **1**    **2**    **3**    **4**    **5**

phytoplankton _____ _____ _____ _____

2 Draw and write the food chain for the text in Activity 1.

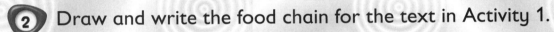

1 → **2** → **3** → **4** → **5**

phytoplankton _____ _____ _____ _____

3 Think about your meals. Answer the questions.

What did you have for breakfast today?
I had _____

Look at this food chain for milk.

| sun → grass → cow → milk |

Write two more food chains for the foods you eat for breakfast.

_____ _____

Write four food chains for your lunch or dinner yesterday.

_____ _____

_____ _____

4 Read and choose the right words.

1 Eagles eat **snakes** / **corn** / **grass**.
2 Snakes eat **flour** / **turtles** / **lizards**.

3 Lizards eat **fish** / **insects** / **birds**.
4 Insects eat **fish** / **plants** / **mice**.

Use your answers to write a land food chain.
plants → _____

5 Sarah is talking to her friend, Katy. What does Katy say to Sarah?

Read the conversation and choose the best answer.
Write a letter (A–E) for each answer.
There is one example.

Example

Sarah:	Hi, Katy! I haven't seen you for a long time.
Katy:	C _____

Questions

1 Sarah: That's nice. Did you go anywhere interesting?
   Katy: _____

2 Sarah: Oh! I haven't been there. Did you like it?
   Katy: _____

3 Sarah: I'll ask my mom to take me next week.
   Katy: _____

4 Sarah: Which is the best day to go, do you think?
   Katy: _____

A   Yes, it was great. There were a lot of things to do.

B   Friday. That's when you can swim with the dolphins.

C   I know. I've been on vacation. (Example)

D   Yes. I went to the Sea Life Center.

E   That's a good idea.

6 Free time

some	any	no	every
someone	**any**one	**no** one	**every**one
something	**any**thing	**no**thing	**every**thing
somewhere	**any**where	**no**where	**every**where

1 Read the test carefully. Follow the instructions.

Reading Test

1 First read ALL the instructions.

2 Write the name of someone you like.

----

3 Think of somewhere you like going.

----

4 Name something you can use to write.

----

5 Write your full name.

----

6 Write somewhere you can sleep.

----

7 Only write the answers to numbers 5 and 8.

----

8 Name someone who teaches you.

----

2 Read and choose the right words.

1 I can't see (**anything**) / **something**.

2 Is there **everywhere** / **anywhere** I can sit down?

3 I couldn't find my book, and I looked **everywhere** / **somewhere**.

4 Can **no one** / **anyone** give me a pencil, please?

5 Do you have **nothing** / **anything** made of plastic?

6 **Everyone** / **Anyone** stand up, please.

3 Read and complete.

anyone	everywhere
everywhere	inside
~~no one~~	no one

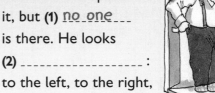

A man is watching TV when he hears the door. He opens it, but **(1)** <u>no one</u> is there. He looks **(2)** _____ : to the left, to the right, and up. Finally he looks down, and he sees a snail. He's angry, so he picks up the snail and throws it really hard. He then goes back **(3)** _____ his house.

    A month later, the same thing happens. He opens the door, but there isn't **(4)** _____ there. He looks **(5)** _____ , but there's **(6)** _____ there. Finally he looks down and sees the snail again. He picks it up, but before he can throw it again, the snail says, 'Why did you do that?'

4 Tell the story in the past. Write it in your notebook.

5 Read and answer.

1 In this sport everyone wears boots. There are 11 players on a team, and anyone can kick something that is round. Not everyone can catch the round thing. Only one player can do that.

a What's the thing that they kick?
  A ball.

b What's the sport? _____

c Who are the people who play this sport?

  _____

2 In this sport someone puts some long things on their feet and goes to the top of a hill or a mountain. They go down the hill over something that is cold and white.

a What are the long things that they put on their feet? _____

b What are they doing? _____

c What's the thing that is cold and white?

  _____

3 In this sport everyone uses something long to hit something that is very small and round. No one can kick, catch, or throw the small round thing. They have to hit it into a small hole.

a What's the sport? _____

b Do you play it inside or outside?

  _____

c Where is the hole? _____

6 Write a definition for a sport or a hobby. Use the words from the "Look" box on Student's Book page 54.

_____
_____
_____
_____
_____

7 Match the sentences with the pictures.

> **a** ~~Would anyone like to play tennis?~~
> **b** Let's go somewhere different on vacation this year.
> **c** No one wants to play soccer today.
> **d** There's nowhere for us to play.

 **1** ☐

 **2** a

 **3** ☐

 **4** ☐

8 Read and order the text.

☐ could do it, but No one did it. Someone was angry, because really it was

☐ do it, but No one thought that Everyone wasn't going to do it.

☐ In the end Everyone was really angry with Someone when No one did what Anyone could do.

1 Once upon a time there were four children in a class. Their names

☐ Their teacher asked for some help in the classroom. Everyone thought that Someone was going to do it. It wasn't difficult, so Anyone

☐ something that Everyone could do. Everyone thought that Anyone could

☐ were No one, Anyone, Someone, and Everyone.

9 Label the pictures.

1 b e a t b o x   2 _ _ _ _ _ _ _ _ _ _ _ _   3 _ _ _ _ _ _ _ _ _ _
4 _ _ _ _ _   5 _ _ _ _ _ _ _ _ _ _ _ _

10 Follow the free time words.

hobby	does	free running	sewing	playing the piano	baseball
fashion design	to	beatbox	Someone	different	chess
skateboarding	places	Ping-Pong	bored	goes	skating
mountain biking	things	cooking	interesting	never	reading
board games	skiing	golf	and	is	who

11 Look at the other words in Activity 10. Use them to write a sentence.

Someone _____

_____

12 Read and answer.

When people first started free running, they did it to get from one place to another using the quickest path. They ran and jumped from wall to wall and down steps. Now they try to do it in the most beautiful way possible.

In Britain, free running became popular in 2003 after someone made a TV show about it.

Free running has also been on a music video by the pop star Madonna. We can see it in action movies and TV commercials, and there is also a free running video game.

It is important to remember that it is something that not everyone can do because free runners need to be very strong and in very good shape. It is also difficult, and it can be dangerous.

1 When did free running become popular in Britain? In 2003. _____
2 Which pop star used free running in her music video? _____
3 Where else can you see free running? _____
4 Can everyone do free running? _____
5 Why / Why not? _____

13 Find four differences.

In picture a, two boys are playing chess. In picture b, they are girls. _____

_____

_____

_____

14 Read the email. Choose the right words and write them on the lines.

Hi, Mary,

How are you? Did **(1)** you___ have a good vacation? **(2)** _____ was great. I went to a special activity camp, and I've started some new hobbies. **(3)** _____ was at the camp for five days, and **(4)** _____ did something different every day! The first two days it was raining, so we did jigsaw puzzles, played board games, and I learned to play chess. I also designed some clothes!

On Wednesday they took **(5)** _____ to the hills, where we rode amazing mountain bikes. It was really exciting. Pete taught **(6)** _____ how to skateboard on Thursday morning, so I spent all afternoon skateboarding with my friends. Friday was **(7)** _____ last day, and we did beatbox and rap!

(8) _____ only problem now is that I have too many hobbies!

Emma

1	they	you	us
2	Mine	I	You
3	He	We	I
4	him	we	them
5	we	they	us
6	me	her	you
7	his	me	our
8	I	Me	My

15 Write questions for the answers.

1 Where did she go? _____
She went to an activity camp.

2 _____
She was there for five days.

3 _____
Because it was raining.

4 _____
She learned to play chess.

5 _____
They rode amazing mountain bikes.

6 _____
They did beatbox and rap.

16 Write an email in your notebook to a friend about your hobbies.

17 Complete the sentences.

cousin	someone	done	~~love~~
doesn't	touch	nothing	country

1 We __love__ going to London.
2 Germany is a big _____ .
3 Can _____ answer this question?
4 Please don't _____ the animals at the zoo.
5 My _____ is coming for lunch.
6 My brother _____ like catching buses.
7 Have you _____ your homework yet?
8 I've opened the box, and there's _____ inside it.

18 🔟 Listen, check, and say.

19 Read the review and answer.

Yesterday I listened to Bruce Star's new single, "Happily Happy."
This is the second song from Bruce's new CD *Bigger*, which
became available at the beginning of February. In my opinion,
this is the best song Bruce has written since he left his old band,
the Starlets. I love the chorus when he repeats "Happily Happy,"
and I think he sings the song beautifully. I also like the drums,
which are strong and loud. The only thing I don't like much is the
sound of the guitar. I think it sounds too fast. I prefer it when he
plays the guitar more slowly.

Expressing opinions
In my opinion …
I like/love …
I think / don't think …
I prefer …

Write it right

1 What's the song called? "Happily Happy." _____
2 Who sang it? _____
3 What album is it from? _____
4 What does the writer like most about it? _____
5 What else does she like? _____
6 What doesn't she like and why? _____

20 Think of your favorite song. Answer the questions in your notebook.

• What's the song called? • Who sang it? • What album is it from?
• What else do you like? • What do you like most? • Is there anything you don't like?

21 Now write a review in your notebook.

I'm going to review

22 **Read and answer.**

1 Where are they going to go?
<u>Somewhere closer to the ocean.</u>

2 What will take Iyam to a cave of gold?

---

3 Are Kukulcan and Quetzalcoatl the same?

---

4 What's Kukulcan's temple called?

---

5 What did the Mayas do before their ball game?

---

6 In what months can you see the snake on the stairs?

---

23 **Look at the code. Write the secret message in your notebook.**

> N = north   S = south   E = east   W = west

Tlachtli – 5E – 4S – 2W – 3N – 3W – 3S – 4E – 4N – 1S – 3W – 3S – 2N – 4E – 2W – 2N – 1W – 4S – 1N – 2W – 5E – 2N – 3W – 1S – 2W – 4E – 1S – 1W – 2W – 3N.

Tlachtli	walls.	ball	rubber	played.	was
that	had	stone	game	They	of
up	pass	high	heavy	in	a
circle	the	a	of	one	made
Mayan	to	through	ball	men	a

? **Do you remember?**

1 Is there <u>anywhere</u> I can sit down?

2 I've looked _____ , but I can't find my pen.

3 _____ is a very old board game.

4 Music and rhythm that you make with your mouth is called _____ .

5 Spain is my favorite _____ .

6 In my _____ , pop music is the best kind of music.

Can do   I can talk about *something, anything, nothing,*
and *everything.*
I can talk about different hobbies.
I can write a song review.

1 Do the music questionnaire.

1 What kind of music do you like? _____

2 How often do you listen to music? _____

3 Who's your favorite singer? _____

4 Which is your favorite group? _____

5 How do you listen to music? (radio, MP3, cell phone, etc.) _____

6 Do you buy music from the Internet? _____

2 Ask someone else the questions. Write about your answers in your notebook.

My dad likes opera, but I don't. We both _____

3 Read and answer the questions.

Louis Armstrong was a famous trumpet player and jazz singer. Louis was born in 1901 in New Orleans in the U.S.A. His family didn't have much money, so after he left school at the age of 11, he sang with a group of boys to get money. He started playing the trumpet at the same age, and at 14, he was working in his first band. During his life, Armstrong played the trumpet and sang with all the world's best musicians. He was famous for his improvisation and the way he played the melodies. In some songs, his singing sounds like a trumpet with no words.

1 What was Louis's last name?
Armstrong. _____

2 When was he born?
_____

3 Where was he born?
_____

4 How old was he when he left school?
_____

5 When did he start playing the trumpet?
_____

6 What was he famous for?
_____

4 Look at this fact sheet for Biz Markie. Write a report.

FACT SHEET

Name: Marcel Hall

Born: April 8, 1964, in New York

School: Long Island High School

First job: DJ in New York clubs –
new name Biz Markie

First record: 1985 single "Def Fresh Crew"

Musical style: hip-hop, rap, and beatbox

Other jobs: actor in the movie "Meteor Man"

Biz Markie's real name _____

5 Read the story. Choose a word from the box. Write the correct word next to numbers 1–5. There is one example.

Example				
~~help~~	them	playing	basement	space
often	plays	want	parents	country

Rachel and Paul help _____ at an animal rescue center in their free time. They (1) _____ go there on weekends. They love (2) _____ with the dogs and cats. They also help take care of (3) _____ . They give the animals their food and clean their boxes. They love doing this because they love animals.

They sometimes go to a special market with their (4) _____ and other grown-ups. At the market they sell things to get money for the rescue center and to ask other people to help. One day a rich and famous actor went to the rescue center and took two big dogs and three cats home to his house in the (5) _____ . He lives in a castle!

(6) Now choose the best name for the story.

Check one box.

Friends and family   ☐

Pet rescue   ☐

A day at the market   ☐

Review Units 5 and 6

1 Read the story. Choose a word from the box. Write the correct word next to numbers 1–5.

> ridden   someone   ~~hobbies~~   chess   cook   nowhere   dangerous
> anything   squid   ocean

Friendly

In today's episode the friends are talking about the <u>hobbies</u> that they do in their free time. Jim's started free running and is really excited about it. He says he got the idea when he saw the movie *The Harder They Run* and the actor, Bruce Willis, had to run through a downtown area. Sally says that she loves action movies and that there are special actors who do all the tricks. Her favorite is Max Limit. Max has driven cars faster than 200 kilometers an hour, he's flown a lot of different planes, and he's **(1)** _____ motorcycles, horses, and elephants. Jenny doesn't find any of this exciting, and she tells Jim that she thinks his new hobby is strange and too **(2)** _____ .

Sue's hobby isn't dangerous, but once when she was painting a small waterfall in the country, she fell into the river, which was moving very fast, and **(3)** _____ had to pull her out. Peter loves trying new things to eat. He says he'll try anything. He's eaten octopus and **(4)** _____ before, but on his last vacation in Japan, he and his parents ate blowfish. This fish is very, very poisonous, and someone has to prepare and cook it very well, or you can die when you eat it. Jenny tries to remember the most dangerous thing she's ever done. Jim laughs because he can't believe she's ever done **(5)** _____ dangerous. Jenny says that once she ate one of Sue's dishes, and everyone knows that she's a terrible cook!

2 Now choose the best name for the story.

Check one box.   Living dangerously ☐   Hard actors ☐   Eating seafood ☐

3 Which is the one that doesn't belong and why?

1 golf (badminton) soccer tennis
<u>You don't play it with a ball.</u> _ _ _ _ _ _ _

2 seen   ridden   walked   thought
_ _

3 baseball   volleyball   soccer   basketball
_ _

4 crab   jellyfish   lobster   turtle
_ _

5 skates   skis   chess   skateboards
_ _

6 laughed   arrived   remembered   turned
_ _

4 Complete the sentences. Count and write the letters.

1 "How many fish has that dolphin
  eaten ?" "Six." `5`

2 In _____ people run
  and jump through a downtown
  area.

3 A sea animal without claws
  that has eight legs. It isn't
  a squid. _____

4 _____ is a black and
  white board game.

5 An _____ is usually
  bigger than seas, rivers,
  and lakes.

6 "Is there _____ in the
  café?" "No, everyone's gone."

7 A _____ is something
  hard on the outside of an
  animal's body. A turtle
  has one.

8 We stand on a _____
  to go fast in parks.

9 A _____ is a round
  animal with eight legs and two
  arms with claws.

10 He's been a soccer player
  _____ 2005.

11 _____ looks like a little
  forest, but it's a lot of sea animals.

12 A _____ is in the same
  family as dolphins and seals,
  but it's much bigger.

13 A bat is _____ that
  we use to hit a ball.

14 "How long have you _____
  your mountain bike?" "A year."

15 He's been a photographer
  _____ nine years.

5 Write the words in the crossword puzzle. Write the message.

1	2	3	3		4	5	6	3		1	7	8	
												n	!

6 Quiz time!

1 What were the people rescuing
  at the beach?
  They were _____

2 Why are plants called "producers"?
  _____

3 What is a top predator?
  _____

4 What is the music behind the tune?
  _____

5 How old is opera?
  _____

7 Write questions for your quiz in your notebook.

63

LOOK again | Possibility

I think it **may look** better with a jacket.　　I **might buy** a new jacket.

I **might not** need a jacket.

1 Write the clothes words in alphabetical order.

pants	~~bracelet~~	sweater	jacket	glasses	dress	watch	coat	skirt
T-shirt	hat	jeans	shirt	purse	shoes	scarf	socks	sneakers

bracelet _____

_____

_____

_____

2 Read and choose the right words.

1 He (**may buy**) / **may buys** / **may to buy** some new sneakers.

2 She **mights wear** / **might wears** / **might wear** her gold bracelet.

3 It **not might** / **might not** / **isn't might** be cold.

4 You **may prefer** / **mays prefer** / **may prefers** olives on your pizza.

5 They **can't might** / **might not** / **don't might** win this afternoon's game.

6 You **might** / **must** / **can** need a scarf because I think it's cold outside!

3 Write about your clothes.

1 My sneakers are made of _____ .

2 My jacket is made of _____ .

3 My shoes _____ .

4 Tomorrow I might wear _____ because _____ .

5 On the weekend I might wear _____ because _____ .

4 Complete the sentences.

| go | visit | ~~wear~~ | get | get up | watch |

1 He might _wear_ a jacket this afternoon because it's cold.

2 She might _____ TV after lunch.

3 They might _____ us today.

4 You might not _____ your present until Sunday.

5 I may not _____ shopping tomorrow.

6 We may _____ early on Saturday.

5 What do you think it is? Use "may."

1 It may be _____

_____

2 _____

_____

3 _____

_____

4 _____

_____

6 Look at the picture. Read and answer "yes" or "no."

1 They might have a picnic. yes_____

2 She might be lost. _____

3 He may want to catch a bus home. _____

4 She might not be happy. _____

5 It might rain. _____

6 They might need coats. _____

7 Correct the sentences.

1 They mights wear their jeans. They might wear their jeans._____

2 She does might take a jacket. _____

3 I don't might put on my sweater. _____

4 Peter may plays soccer tomorrow. _____

5 I might not to wear my black shoes. _____

6 They mays wear their new sneakers. _____

8 Find and write five sentences.

Susan	might put	is green	coats and scarves.
Our school	took	of	and red.
Richard	uniform	on their	plastic.
My school bag's	wore her	blue spotted	with him.
The children	made	a jacket	belt.

1 Susan wore her blue spotted belt._____

2 _____

3 _____

4 _____

5 _____

9 Find two words for each group of letters. One is a clothes word.

1 sn- ~~sneakers~~ , ~~snack~~
2 sh- _____ , _____
3 po- _____ , _____
4 gl- _____ , _____
5 u-   _____ , _____
6 bu- _____ , _____

mbrella

oves

~~eakers~~

ue

gly

tter

orts

~~ack~~

opping

tato

cket

tton

10 Label the pictures with words from Activity 9.

pocket _____ _____ _____ _____ _____ _____

11 Read and complete the sentences with 1, 2, 3, or 4 words.

Last Saturday, Jane went shopping with her Aunt Helen to buy some new clothes. They went to three different clothing stores. The first store was called Legs Eleven, and they had a lot of socks. Jane chose some gray and green ones.

Next they went to look for some shorts. They found a lot in a store called 4 Fashion. Jane didn't know which ones to choose, so her aunt helped her. She got a nice blue pair made of cotton, with big pockets.

In the last clothing store, they bought a beautiful red coat. She didn't buy any new sneakers because she has three pairs at home. When they were coming home, it started to rain, so they bought two umbrellas from a small store. They caught the bus home because they didn't want to get wet.

1 Jane went shopping with her Aunt Helen. _____
2 Legs Eleven was _____ store that they went in.
3 Jane's new socks are _____ .
4 Aunt Helen helped Jane _____ some shorts.
5 Jane's new blue shorts are made of _____ , and they have big pockets.
6 She didn't need _____ because she has three pairs.
7 They got _____ in the last clothing store.
8 They went home on _____ because it was raining.

12 Read and complete the circle with names and clothes words.

Three girls and two boys are sitting around a table. Richard is sitting between two girls. The girl on his left is Emma.

The girl on William's left is Betty.

The girl between Richard and Sarah is wearing a striped T-shirt and a skirt. She has a beautiful gold ring.

The boy with the shorts is wearing a belt. He's also wearing a shirt and a new jacket.

The girl with the scarf isn't wearing a skirt. She's wearing some pants and a sweater that is made of cotton.

The girl on the right of Richard has some plastic earrings on. She's also wearing a striped sweater, a skirt, and sneakers.

The other boy is cold, so he's wearing some gloves. His sweater is striped, and he's also wearing pants.

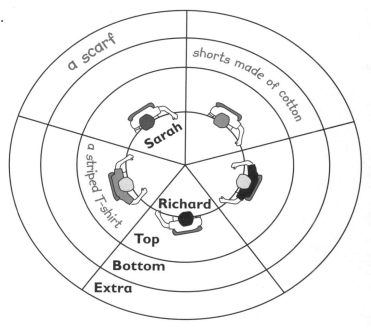

13 Draw a piece of clothing and write about it.

These are my favorite long shorts. They're very, very big, so I wear them with a belt. They're dark brown, and they have big pockets on the legs above the knees. My mom hates them, but I love them!

14 Describe the picture.

1 No one is playing chess. _____
2 Nothing _____
_____ .
3 No one _____
_____ .
4 Everyone _____
_____ .

15 Match the sentences with the pictures. Write letters a–f.

> **a** I'm angry. Please stop talking!   **b** ~~I'm on vacation. I'm happy!~~
> **c** I'm excited! This is a fantastic present!   **d** What a surprise!
> **e** I'm tired. Good night, Mom.   **f** I'm sad. I've hurt my knee.

16 Listen, check, and say.

17 Look at the pictures. Read and check (✓) the correct picture.

There are two people in the picture: a man and a woman. The man is taller than the woman, but she has longer hair. The man has dark curly hair and a small beard, but he doesn't have a mustache. He's wearing a long coat over the top of a pair of black pants and a shirt. He has black shoes on. He looks like a detective. He's standing next to a woman who has long, curly, blond hair. She has big eyes and a long thin nose. She's smiling. She's wearing jeans, a short jacket, and sneakers. She looks like a rock star.

Describing people
Describe their face and body.
➜ He has a big nose and long, brown, curly hair.
Describe their clothes.
➜ She's wearing a beautiful, long, blue cotton skirt.
Describe what they look like.
➜ He looks like an angry chef.

Write it right

18 Now write a description in your notebook of one of the other pictures. Can your friend guess which picture it is?

19 Read and answer.

1 What did Aztec braves wear? _They wore birds' feathers and animal fur._

2 How did everyone feel when they saw them? _____

3 What did the Mayas do in the round building? _____

4 Why do they have to move fast? _____

5 When do the bowls work like mirrors? _____

6 At what time is the Sun at its highest? _____

20 Put the verbs into the simple past.

The Aztecs **(1)** _were_ (are) very rich. They **(2)** _____ (have) fields and water to grow plants for food and materials. They also **(3)** _____ (have) a lot of stone for building, gold, and silver. Like the Mayas, they **(4)** _____ (get) the liquid from rubber trees and **(5)** _____ (use) that, too. They **(6)** _____ (make) balls for their famous ball game and **(7)** _____ (use) it to brush their teeth after meals. They **(8)** _____ (invent) the first chewing gum! Rich Aztec people **(9)** _____ (wear) more clothes than poor people, and their clothes **(10)** _____ (are) made from different cloth. Poor people **(11)** _____ (can't) wear cotton. Women and girls **(12)** _____ (make) most of their cloth from the "century plant" and **(13)** _____ (use) bright colors and designs to decorate it. They **(14)** _____ (make) shoes from rubber, but if they **(15)** _____ (have) to go into a temple or see the king, they **(16)** _____ (can't) wear anything on their feet. When they **(17)** _____ (dance), they **(18)** _____ (wear) belts with seashells to make music as they **(19)** _____ (move). They sometimes **(20)** _____ (wear) feathers and animal fur, too. Aztec braves **(21)** _____ (paint) their faces to look horrible and to make people afraid of them. Married women **(22)** _____ (put) their hair up on top of their heads. Corn **(23)** _____ (is) their most important food, but they also **(24)** _____ (eat) a lot of vegetables. They **(25)** _____ (don't eat) a lot of meat, but they sometimes **(26)** _____ (eat) insects and lizards.

? **Do you remember?**

1 It might _rain_ later, so I'm going to take an umbrella.

2 I need to study because we _____ have a math test tomorrow, but I'm not sure.

3 I have a new _____ , so my pants don't fall down.

4 When it's cold, I wear _____ on my hands.

5 My brother is very _____ because it's his birthday party tonight.

6 That man with the long coat looks _____ a detective.

Can do   I can talk about possibility using *may* and *might*.

I can talk about clothes.

I can write a description of someone and their clothes.

1 Label the picture.

belt	gloves	jacket
~~scarf~~	pocket	helmet
pants	boots	

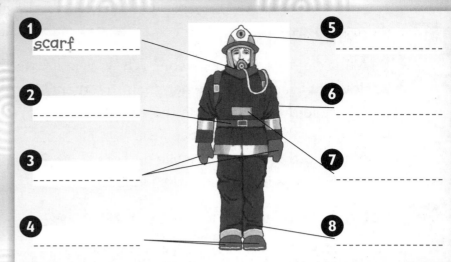

1 scarf _____

2 _____

3 _____

4 _____

5 _____

6 _____

7 _____

8 _____

2 Complete the text about the firefighter's uniform. Use words from Activity 1.

This firefighter's uniform is made from special materials to protect him at work. The **(1)** helmet_____ hasn't changed much in the last 150 years. It is made of leather, and it protects the firefighter's head.

　　Below his face, the firefighter wears a **(2)** _____. It's made of cotton, and he can pull it up over his head in a fire.

　　The firefighter's jacket has a special **(3)** _____ at the front. He uses this to carry his radio or his gloves.

　　The firefighter wears **(4)** _____ that are bigger than usual. He must put them on quickly over his boots when he needs to go and fight a fire. They have a plastic stripe at the bottom so people can see him in the dark. His **(5)** _____ are made of leather and metal. They are very strong.

　　One of the most important parts of the firefighter's uniform is his **(6)** _____. They are made of leather and they protect his hands.

3 Label the activities and sports. Write about two of the uniforms.

1 　**2** 　**3** 　**4**　**5**

dancing_____　_____　_____　_____

This man is wearing special clothes for playing sports.

Listen and check (✓) the box. There is one example.

What has Holly put on to go to the park?

A ✓   B ☐   C ☐

1   Where has Richard left his umbrella?

 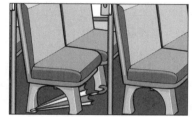 

A ☐   B ☐   C ☐

2   Where's William going to go for his vacation?

 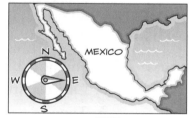 

A ☐   B ☐   C ☐

3   Which pants will Emma wear to the party?

A ☐   B ☐   C ☐

4   Where did Helen find her belt?

A ☐   B ☐   C ☐

LOOK again — Present perfect and adverbs

Have you finished **yet**?	I've **just** finished this book.
I haven't finished **yet**.	I've **already** finished my project.

1 Find two irregular past participles for each group of letters.

1 b- _been_ , _begun_
2 m- ____ , ____
3 dr- ____ , ____
4 t- ____ , ____
5 th- ____ , ____
6 br- ____ , ____

7 sp- ____ , ____
8 l- ____ , ____
9 c- ____ , ____
10 st- ____ , ____
11 r- ____ , ____
12 go- ____ , ____

aken   awn   ost   tten   oken   idden   et   iven

aught   ome   ood   ought   eant   ent   ~~een~~   eft

olen   aught   rown   un   oken   t   ought   ~~egun~~

2 Complete the sentences with verbs from Activity 1.

1 He's r_idden_ his bike for two hours.
2 They've just g____ out.
3 This is the third time I've b____ to read this book!
4 She hasn't s____ all her money yet.
5 Our cat still hasn't c____ home.
6 They've just d____ a picture.

3 Look at the picture. Write sentences.

1 (get up) _He's already gotten up._
2 (clean his room) _He hasn't cleaned his room yet._
3 (make his bed) ____
4 (put on his shoes) ____
5 (have breakfast) ____
6 (put on his pants) ____

Come on! Time for breakfast!

4 Write sentences about you today. Use "already," "yet," or "just."

1 (have lunch) _I've already had lunch. / I haven't had lunch yet. / I've just had lunch._
2 (read something) ____
3 (do some of my homework) ____
4 (listen to music) ____

5 Check (✓) two more correct sentences. Correct two more sentences.

1 "Clean your room!" "I've already cleaned it!" ✓ _____
2 He is done his homework already.   *He's already done his homework.*
3 Has he been to Australia?   _____
4 I live here for ten years.   _____
5 They's seen that movie already.   _____
6 She's studied English for three years.   _____

6 What have they just done?

He's just cleaned his room.   She_____.   They_____.

She_____.   We_____.   He_____.

7 Look at the Hirds' plans. Read and answer "Yes, they have" or "No, they haven't."

VACATION!		morning	afternoon
Monday	Cambridge	see the university	play in a park
Tuesday	Nottingham	see the castle	walk in Sherwood Forest
Wednesday	Liverpool	cross the River Mersey	go shopping
Thursday	York	walk on the Roman walls	visit the Viking Museum
Friday	London	visit the Science Museum	see Big Ben

Now it is Wednesday lunchtime.

1 The Hirds haven't been to Cambridge yet.   *Yes, they have.*
2 They have already seen Nottingham Castle.   _____
3 They have already been shopping in Liverpool.   _____
4 They haven't visited the Science Museum yet.   _____
5 They've already walked in Sherwood Forest.   _____
6 They haven't played in a park in Cambridge yet.   _____

8 Label the car stickers with nationalities. Use the letters in the box.

(E) (BR)

```
e a a a a a c c d
e e e e e e e g h
h i i i i k l m n
n n n n n o p r
r r r r s s t u u x
z B F G G I M P S
```

(IND) (F)

1 Spanish _____ 2 _____ 5 _____ 6 _____

(GR) (P) (D) (MEX)

3 _____ 4 _____ 7 _____ 8 _____

9 What countries are these web pages from?

www.mundocrianças.br	1 Brazil _____	www.kidsofindia.in	5 _____
www.kinderhere.de	2 _____	www.sunfun4kids.gr	6 _____
www.niñolandia.es	3 _____	www.4crianças.pt	7 _____
www.mondenfant.fr	4 _____	www.mundoniños.mx	8 _____

10 Read and answer.

Did you know that there are 195 countries in the world? Each of them has a capital city. Some of them even have more than one capital, and South Africa has three capitals! Some capitals aren't difficult to learn. For example, it's easy to remember that Mexico City is the capital of Mexico and that Brasilia is the capital of Brazil. We know the names of other capitals because we hear about them in history class, on the news, and from sporting events.

You might know that the capital of Spain is Madrid, and the capital of Greece is Athens. You may even know that the German capital is Berlin, and that the Portuguese capital is Lisbon, but did you know that the Indian capital is New Delhi? Some capitals surprise us because they aren't the biggest city in the country. Did you know that the capital of Australia isn't Sydney? No, it's Canberra, and the capital of the U.S.A. isn't New York. It's Washington, D.C.

1 What is the Mexican capital? Mexico City. _____
2 What is the capital of India? _____
3 Which country is Canberra the capital of? _____
4 What's the name of the Greek capital? _____
5 What is the Spanish capital? _____
6 What's the capital of Portugal? _____
7 Which country is Washington, D.C. the capital of? _____
8 What is the Brazilian capital? _____

11 Complete the words with the groups of letters in the box. Use each group for only one pair of words.

sh	~~me~~	any	ey	co	al	try	ch	tal	th

1 Ro...   me_____ ...tal   Yes (No)
2 Turk... _____ ...es   Yes No
3 coun... _____ ...ing   Yes No
4 Germ... _____ ...where   Yes No
5 Fren... _____ ...opsticks   Yes No

6 Portug... _____ ...ready   Yes No
7 capi... _____ ...lest   Yes No
8 Engli... _____ ...orts   Yes No
9 nor... _____ ...rown   Yes No
10 Mexi... _____ ...mb   Yes No

12 Say the pairs of words in Activity 11. Do the letters sound the same in both words? Circle "Yes" or "No."

Rome ... metal

13 Ask and answer. Write your friend's answers.

1 Have you ever eaten Spanish food? _____   What was it? _____
2 Have you ever eaten Mexican food? _____   What was it? _____
3 Have you ever eaten Indian food? _____   What was it? _____
4 Have you ever eaten Portuguese food? _____   What was it? _____
5 Have you ever eaten Italian food? _____   What was it? _____
6 Have you ever eaten Greek food? _____   What was it? _____
7 Have you ever eaten _____ food? _____   What was it? _____
8 Have you ever eaten _____ food? _____   What was it? _____

14 Write a report about international food that you and your friend have eaten.

We haven't eaten Greek food, but I have eaten Portuguese food. I can't remember the word, but it was fish with tomatoes. It was delicious. Igor has eaten Mexican food. He had

15 Complete the lists.

| foggy | ~~shorts~~ | keyboards | gold | cookies | flashlights | science | went |

1 Shirts, skirts, sneakers, and _shorts_ .
2 Butter, jelly, sauce, popcorn, and _____ .
3 English, geography, art, math, and _____ .
4 Leather, metal, wool, and _____ .
5 Lived, wanted, wished, and _____ .
6 Sunny, cloudy, windy, and _____ .
7 Laptops, webcams, headphones, and _____ .
8 Tents, backpacks, sleeping bags, and _____ .

16 Listen, check, and say.

17 Write these words in order of size from the biggest to the smallest.

| city | continent | country | Earth | street | our solar system |
| town | ~~the universe~~ | village |

the universe _____

_____

18 Read and complete Robert's form.

Woman: How can I help you?
Robert: I'd like to go on your Summer English Course in England.
Woman: Fine. Now I need some information to put on the form. First, your name and last name, please.
Robert: Robert Schmidt.
Woman: OK, and when were you born?
Robert: On June 15, 1996.
Woman: Where are you from?
Robert: I'm from Germany.
Woman: And your address, please?
Robert: I live at 35 Bear Street, Berlin.
Woman: What's the ZIP code?
Robert: I think it's 10117.
Woman: Good. And finally, what's your telephone number?
Robert: Um, 689-730241.

Completing a form
• Read the headings carefully.
• Does the form want you to use CAPITAL letters?
• Do you have to circle or check anything?

Write it right

Please use CAPITAL letters.
First name: ROBERT _____
Last name: _____
Course (please circle): Music / Art / English / P.E.
Date of birth: _____
Country of birth: _____
Nationality: _____
Address: _____
ZIP code: _____
Telephone number: _____

19 Read and answer.

1 What's Iyam just done? <u>He's just pushed the corn symbol.</u>

2 How long has the museum at Balankanche been open? _____

3 How did the Mayas water their fields? _____

4 How long have Interpol wanted Iyam and Richard Tricker? _____

5 What are Sir Doug Bones and Diggory going to do with the Sun Stone? _____

6 What did Emily's grandfather use to follow them? _____

20 Do the Mayan quiz. True (T) or False (F)?

1 The Aztecs built the modern-day Mexico City on a lake called Texcoco because they saw a Quetzal bird there. **T / (F)**

2 The Mayas studied the Sun, the Moon, and the stars to measure time. **T / F**

3 Gold was the most important material in the Aztecs' lives. **T / F**

4 The Mayas used picture writing, or "glyphs," to communicate by writing. **T / F**

5 The Mayas played musical instruments. Some of these were made of turtle shells, wood, and seashells. **T / F**

6 The Pyramid of Kukulcan sounds like a Quetzal bird singing when someone climbs it. **T / F**

7 The Mayas played a ballgame called "tlachtli." It's like a cross between modern volleyball and basketball. **T / F**

8 Aztec braves painted their faces and wore birds' feathers and animal fur to look beautiful and to make people love them. **T / F**

9 The first chewing gum was made from soft rubber from trees. The Mayas used it to brush their teeth. **T / F**

10 The form of a snake moves up and down the north stairs of the Pyramid of the Sun: up in March and down in September. **T / F**

Answers:
1 False. Because they saw an eagle there and thought it was a sign from their gods.
3 False. Quetzal feathers were more important than gold.
6 False. This happens when someone claps hands.
8 False. They painted their faces and wore these things to look horrible and to make people feel afraid of them.

? Do you remember?

1 It's seven o'clock in the evening. Have you done your homework <u>yet?</u>_____

2 Yes, I've _____ finished it! I finished it ten seconds ago.

3 Paris is the _____ of France.

4 People in Mexico speak _____.

5 I have been to Germany, France, and Spain, but I can't speak _____, _____ or _____.

6 "What _____ are you?" "I'm Portuguese."

Can do
I can talk about what has already or just happened and what hasn't happened yet.
I can talk about different countries and nationalities.
I can complete a form in English.

77

1 Complete the text with words from the box.

| Chinese | started | ~~book~~ | people | Russia | important | years |

This **(1)** _book_ is in the Latin alphabet. The people of Rome in Italy **(2)** _____ using the Latin alphabet more than 2,700 **(3)** _____ ago. Now more than two billion **(4)** _____ use it.

There are also a lot of other **(5)** _____ alphabets. After the Latin alphabet, the next most popular ways of writing are the Chinese script and the Devanagari alphabet from India. About 1.2 billion people use the **(6)** _____ script and 1 billion use the Devanagari alphabet. Then there is the Arabic alphabet, which is used by half a billion (500 million) people, and the Cyrillic alphabet. There are about 300 million people from Central and Eastern Europe, for example, in **(7)** _____ , who use the Cyrillic alphabet. There are a lot of other ways of writing, too.

2 Read again and answer.

1 What alphabet are you using to answer this question? _The Latin alphabet._

2 How old is it? _____

3 How many people use it today? _____

4 What alphabet do Indian people use? _____

5 What is the name of the other alphabet from Central and Eastern Europe? _____

6 How many people write in it? _____

3 Where are these English words from? Label the map.

| kiwi | kangaroo | karate | ~~igloo~~ | opera | athlete | chocolate |

1 _igloo_

2 _____

3 _____

Greenland

Italy

Greece

Mexico

Japan

Australia

New Zealand

4 _____

5 _____

6 _____

7 _____

4 Think of a word from your language that you would like to give to English. Write a letter to a dictionary writer saying why they should add this word to the dictionary.

5 Read the diary and write the missing words. Write one word on each line.

Friday, April 4

Example	This evening I'm writing in my diary ....in............ Paris!
1	Paris is the capital of .... I am here because I
2	want to learn to .... French better and to see
3	the city, of course. Today I .... to the Eiffel
	Tower with my friends. It's really tall, and it looks very
4	beautiful. I .... some great pictures.
5	Tomorrow we're .... to visit a famous museum,
	the Louvre, so we can see the *Mona Lisa*. I can't wait!

Review Units 7 and 8

1 Read the story. Choose a word from the box. Write the correct word next to numbers 1–5.

| umbrellas | ~~just~~ | worn | Paris | belt | same | pockets | Spanish | capital | button |

Friendly

Dan, Alex, and Maria are sad because the second series of *Friendly* has *just*_____ ended. They all agree that the funniest episode of this series was "Jim's new clothes."

In this episode Jim and Peter went to London to buy some new clothes. They caught the train to the **(1)** _____ one Saturday morning. They found a store called Fine Fashion. The salesman told them that all the clothes came from **(2)** _____ , the capital of France and the capital of fashion.

Jim bought some big green pants with **(3)** _____ above the knees. He bought a light gray T-shirt and a black **(4)** _____ . He liked his new clothes, and he decided to wear them home.

When they went back to the station, they saw Jim's grandfather, but it was very funny because his grandpa's pants were big and green with pockets above the knees. He was also wearing a light gray T-shirt and a black belt. His clothes were the **(5)** _____ as Jim's.

2 Now choose the best name for the story.

Check one box.   Streets ahead ☐   Capital cities ☐   The latest fashion ☐

3 Read and match the jokes.

1 What do you call an elephant at the North Pole?
2 What did the scarf say to the hat?
3 Why do birds fly south in the winter?
4 What do we have to break before we can use it?
5 What kind of key opens a banana?
6 What do you get if you cross a kangaroo with an elephant?
7 What do you call an elephant with a carrot in each ear?
8 What do sea monsters eat?
9 How far can you walk into the woods?
10 What's the best thing to put into ice cream?

a Anything you want because it can't hear you!
b A monkey!
c A spoon!
d Lost!
e Because it's easier than walking!
f Half way. Then you're walking out of the woods.
g You go on ahead, I'll just hang around.
h Big holes in Australia!
i An egg.
j Fish and ships.

☐
☐
☐
1
☐
☐
☐
☐

4 Complete the sentences. Count and write the letters.

1 <u>Shorts</u> are short pants. We wear them in summer. **6**

2 Hindi, French, and Portuguese are different _____ .

3 We wear _____ on our hands.

4 A hundred years is a _____ .

5 He's just _____ his coat on. He's going out.

6 Africa is a _____ .

7 You might have a _____ inside your jacket. You can carry things in it.

8 The cities of London, Paris, and Rome are all _____ .

9 We use this to close our shirts and coats. It can be different shapes and colors. _____

10 We wear a _____ at the top of our pants or jeans, so they don't fall down.

11 "What _____ is she?" "She's Chinese."

12 Oh, no! It's just started to rain and I've left my _____ at home!

13 Special clothes to protect us. A firefighter wears one. _____

5 Now complete the crossword puzzle. Write the message.

1	2	3	4	5	6		7	4	6	7
							h			h

!

6 Quiz time!

1 Why was Dan's shirt funny at the disco?
<u>It was</u> _____

2 How long have people in China worn Han clothes? _____

3 What are moccasins? _____

4 How many countries won the ezine competition? _____

5 Where is sushi from? _____

6 What does the prefix "tele-" mean? _____

7 Write questions for your quiz in your notebook.

1 Write sentences with "should" or "shouldn't."

1 be careful / chat / Internet <u>You should be careful when you chat on the Internet.</u>

2 spend / more than an hour a day / a computer screen _____

3 be afraid / use technology _____

4 play exciting computer games / before / bed _____

5 get angry / you can't use a computer _____

2 Read and answer.

David's older sister, Jenny, thinks he has a problem with computers. He spends more than two hours a day in front of the screen, and he's very unhappy when he doesn't have an internet connection. He spends all weekend at home playing on the computer, and he doesn't want to go out with his friends. When his parents call him for family meals, he takes about 10 minutes to go to the table. Then he gets angry when he has to help the family clean up after the meal. He only wants to go back to the computer. Last Sunday, Jenny saw him playing games on the computer at three o'clock in the morning when the family was all in bed.

1 Who thinks David has a problem? <u>Jenny</u> _____

2 How much time does he spend on the computer every day? _____

3 Why doesn't he want to go out with his friends? _____

4 What was he doing at three o'clock in the morning last Sunday? _____

5 Do you think David has a problem? _____

6 What do you think Jenny should do? _____

_____

Be safe at home

1 Read and choose the answer.

How safe are you?

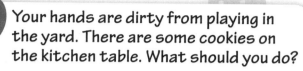

1 Your hands are dirty from playing in the yard. There are some cookies on the kitchen table. What should you do?

a Clean your hands on your pants and take a cookie.
b Eat two cookies quickly before your little sister comes.
c Wash your hands and then have a cookie.

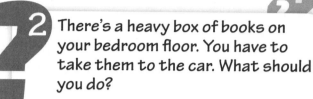

2 There's a heavy box of books on your bedroom floor. You have to take them to the car. What should you do?

a Put the books into two boxes and carry the first one, then the other to the car.
b Pick up the box. It's difficult, but you try to take it very quickly.
c Ask your little sister to carry the box for you.

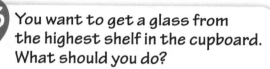

3 You want to get a glass from the highest shelf in the cupboard. What should you do?

a Climb onto a chair and put your hands above your head to get it.
b Ask your mom or dad to help you.
c Pick up your little brother and put him on your shoulders, so he can get it for you.

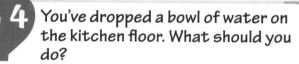

4 You've dropped a bowl of water on the kitchen floor. What should you do?

a Dry the floor carefully because it's dangerous to walk on.
b Go outside and play. Somebody else can clean it.
c Put a chair over the water so nobody can see it.

2 Write a safety contract for your home.

1 _We must put our toys away safely._____
2 _____
3 _____
4 _____
5 _____

Safety at home

_____ got the Safety at Home certificate.

Congratulations!

1 **Read and choose the right words.**

Last month I went to a small **(1) country / city / (village)** in Africa and watched how families worked together. In these families, the children help their parents, and **(2) everyone / everywhere / anyone** works. For example, if there are three children, the oldest takes care **(3) off / at / of** the youngest when the parents are working. The other child stays with the family animals, like goats or sheep. Every day the two older **(4) parents / children / animals** get the water. They have **(5) got / to / at** walk two kilometers to get it.

They don't have a TV, a computer, or a lot of **(6) free / the / good** time, but I found that they're **(7) happy / happier / happiest** than some children in different countries who have all these things.

2 **Write about how you help at home. Use the pictures and questions to help you.**

What jobs do you do at home?
What jobs do your mom, dad, brothers, and sisters do?
Do you enjoy doing jobs at home? Why? Why not?
How do you feel when you help at home?

	At home, I do several things to help. I

1 Read and answer.

1 There's a new boy in school. How can you help him make friends?

----

2 Some children in school have started calling you horrible names. What should you do?

----

3 Your little brother has a big problem in school. He's asked you not to tell anybody. You think the problem is serious. What are you going to do?

----

4 Your group of friends in school don't like a girl. They've told you not to go out with this girl, or they won't talk to you. What should you do?

----

5 One of your friends has sent some horrible messages to another student in school. What are you going to do?

----

2 Talk about your ideas with your friend. Do you agree?

(I agree.)   (I don't agree. I think …)

3 Read and match.

1 I'm very	a I do?	
2 They think	b angry.	1
3 This isn't	c very worried.	
4 What should	d help me.	
5 I'm	e the first time.	
6 Please	f it's funny.	

4 Imagine you have a problem at home or school. Write a letter to Betty and Robert. Use phrases from Activity 3 to help you.

5 Swap letters with a friend. Read your friend's letter and give him/her some advice.

(You should/shouldn't …)   (You have to …)

(The best idea is to …)   (You must / must not …)

85

Grammar reference

Complete the sentences.

should ~~Would~~ Should Let's must not don't

1 _Would_ you like some ice cream?
2 You _____ play soccer in the road.
3 Why _____ we send her a text message?
4 _____ we chat online?
5 I _____ do my homework before I play on the computer.
6 _____ write an article for the ezine.

1 Write questions. Answer.

1 He / be an actor? (✗) _Is he going to be an actor?_ _No, he isn't._
2 They / see a movie? (✓) _____
3 You / do your homework? (✓) _____
4 She / be in the play? (✗) _____
5 We / play tennis? (✗) _____
6 He / read a book about dragons? (✓) _____

2 Read and write.

1 They'll go to the Moon by plane. (rocket) _No, they won't. They'll go there by rocket._
2 She'll eat fruit. (special food) _____
3 I'll wear jeans. (skirt) _____
4 They'll fly to Jupiter. (Mars) _____
5 We'll leave next week. (next month) _____
6 There'll be a lot of people. (robots) _____

3 Read and match.

1 I was snowboarding
2 They were waiting at the bus
3 She was making bread
4 We were having a picnic when
5 I was walking through the
6 He was sleeping when he

a felt a mouse in his sleeping bag.
b forest when I dropped my flashlight.
c when she lost her ring.
d when I fell and hurt my elbow. | 1 |
e the storm began.
f stop when they saw their friend.

4 Read and circle the answer.

1 There are too (many) / any knives.
2 There isn't / aren't enough chairs.
3 She doesn't have much / many sugar.
4 They don't have too / enough forks.
5 Did they have much / many cookies?
6 How many / much pasta do you want?

5 Complete the sentences. Write *for* or *since*.

1 She's had her computer <u>since</u> 2011.
2 We've studied English _____ five years.
3 I haven't played tennis _____ two weeks.
4 They've lived here _____ they were six.
5 He's been at his new school _____ three months.
6 She hasn't seen Peter _____ the summer.

6 Complete the sentences.

> somewhere   no one   anything   something   ~~Everything~~   any

1 It's raining. <u>Everything</u> in the yard is wet.
2 I saw _____ interesting on TV last night.
3 The house was empty because _____ was at home.
4 He didn't have _____ money, so he didn't go to the movies.
5 I want to go _____ exciting on vacation this year.
6 Our town is really boring for young people. There isn't _____ to do.

7 Read and order the words.

1 (go to) (this evening) (We might) (the movies)

<u>We might go to the movies this evening.</u>

2 (I'm tired) (leave the disco) (I may) (early because)

_____

3 (They may not) (their project) (have time) (to finish)

_____

8 Write the sentences in the present perfect. Use the words given.

1 (just) I arrive at the airport.   <u>I've just arrived at the airport.</u>
2 (yet) He not be to New York.   _____
3 (already) I clean my room.   _____
4 (yet) you write that email?   _____
5 (just) He wake up.   _____
6 (already) They finish the book.   _____

Irregular verbs

Infinitive	Past tense	Past participle
be	was / were	been
be called	was / were called	been called
be going to	was / were going to	been going to
begin	began	begun
break	broke	broken
bring	brought	brought
buy	bought	bought
can	could	could
catch	caught	caught
choose	chose	chosen
come	came	come
cut	cut	cut
do	did	done
draw	drew	drawn
drink	drank	drunk
drive	drove	driven
dry	dried	dried
eat	ate	eaten
fall	fell	fallen
fall over	fell over	fallen over
feel	felt	felt
find	found	found
find out	found out	found out
fly	flew	flown
forget	forgot	forgotten
get	got	gotten
get (un)dressed	got (un)dressed	gotten (un)dressed
get (up / on / off)	got (up / on / off)	gotten (up / on / off)
get to	got to	gotten to
give	gave	given
go	went	gone
go out	went out	gone out
go shopping	went shopping	gone shopping
grow	grew	grown
have	had	had
have to	had to	had to
hear	heard	heard
hide	hid	hidden
hit	hit	hit
hold	held	held
hurt	hurt	hurt
keep	kept	kept
know	knew	known

Infinitive	Past tense	Past participle
leave	left	left
let	let	let
lie down	lay down	lain down
lose	lost	lost
make	made	made
make sure	made sure	made sure
mean	meant	meant
meet	met	met
must	had to	had to
put	put	put
put on	put on	put on
read	read	read
ride	rode	ridden
run	ran	run
say	said	said
see	saw	seen
sell	sold	sold
send	sent	sent
sing	sang	sung
sit	sat	sat
sleep	slept	slept
speak	spoke	spoken
spend	spent	spent
stand	stood	stood
steal	stole	stolen
swim	swam	swum
swing	swung	swung
take	took	taken
take a picture	took a picture	taken a picture
take off	took off	taken off
teach	taught	taught
tell	told	told
think	thought	thought
throw	threw	thrown
understand	understood	understood
wake up	woke up	woken up
wear	wore	worn
win	won	won
write	wrote	written

My languages

All languages are fantastic!

This portfolio is to help you learn English. You can add more pages about learning English or other languages.

How many languages do you know?

Do you want to learn other languages?

Language: _____

Where I speak this language: _____

Who I speak it with: _____

Check (✓). In this language I also …

listen to music ☐   watch movies ☐

read books and magazines ☐   write letters/emails ☐

Language: _____

Where I speak this language: _____

Who I speak it with: _____

Check (✓). In this language I also …

listen to music ☐   watch movies ☐

read books and magazines ☐   write letters/emails ☐

Language: _____

Where I speak this language: _____

Who I speak it with: _____

Check (✓). In this language I also …

listen to music ☐   watch movies ☐

read books and magazines ☐   write letters/emails ☐

Other languages I know: _____

_____

Are there any languages you want to learn in the future?

_____

_____

Language Portfolio language skills: My progress

What can you do in English in the classroom?   Date: _____

Skill	What I can do	I can do it easily: ✓✓ I can do it: ✓ I want more practice: !!
Listening	**I can understand questions about:** • me and my family • where I live • what I do in school and in my free time • what I like and don't like	
	In the classroom I can understand: • when my teacher asks me to do things in class and tells me what I need to do • when I listen to the *Kid's Box* CD	
Reading	**I can understand English words and sentences:** • when the teacher writes on the board • in my *Kid's Box* Student's Book and Workbook • when I read books at my English level	
Speaking	**Talking with another person. I can:** • talk about myself and my family • say what I do in school and in my free time • talk about some of the topics in the Student's Book	
	Talking to the class. I can: • talk about my favorite things (food, animals, and sports) • talk about a project we did in class	
Writing	**I can write:** • about myself and the things I do • about my family and where I live • a story or about something that I did • a short letter or an email to a friend	

Teacher's comments: _____

I can ...   Units 1 and 2

	I can do it easily: ✓✓ I can do it: ✓ I want more practice: !!

1 Listening. I can understand people when they're talking about what they're going to do.

I'm going to audition for the school play.

School Play
The Lion King
Actors needed
Auditions
Wednesday 3:45

That's great! Can we come, too?

1	

2 Speaking. I can talk about what I'm going to do next weekend.

movies

I'm going to the movies with my mom and dad next weekend.

2	

3 Reading. I can understand the Diggory Bones comic book in the *Kid's Box* Student's Book.

Good work!

3	

4 Writing. I can write about my future using *will*.

4	

In 2050, I'll be forty-five years old.
I'll ...

I can ...   # Units 3 and 4

	I can do it easily: ✓✓ I can do it: ✓ I want more practice: !!
	1
	2
	3
	4

1 🎧 Listening. I can understand a story someone tells me using the past tense.

> I was climbing over a rock when I fell.

2 💬 Speaking. I can ask and answer questions to find out what the people in my class were doing yesterday or last weekend.

> Were you sleeping at 11 o'clock last night?

> Yes, I was.

3 🔍 Reading. I can read about what people in different countries eat.

4 ✏️ Writing. I can write about food. I can write a recipe, invent a story about food, or write about food in my country.

	Our food is very nice. We eat a lot of rice and vegetables.

I can ...   # Units 5 and 6

	can do it easily: ✓✓ I can do it: ✓ I want more practice: !!
	1
	2
	3
	4

1 Listening. I can understand people talking about a recent event using the present perfect.

The people have found some dolphins at the beach.

2 Speaking. I can talk about important things that have happened in my life.

I've lived in this city since I was eight years old. My little sister was born in 2013.

3 Reading. I can read about people and their hobbies.

4 Writing. I can write about my hobbies and what I like to do in my free time.

In my free time I like to be outside ...

I can ... Units 7 and 8

I can do it easily: ✓✓ I can do it: ✓ I want more practice: !!
1
2
3
4

1 Listening. I can understand when people describe clothes.

He's wearing a striped sweater.

2 Speaking. I can talk about the clothes I'm wearing and the clothes I wear for different activities.

I'm wearing my school uniform now, but when I play soccer I wear a T-shirt, shorts, and special shoes.

3 Reading. I can read about different countries and find the important information.

The French have the most famous bike race in the world. It's called the Tour de France.

4 Writing. I can write about what I've done this year.

This year I've ..., but I haven't ...

My learning diary:
What I learned in class

1 Some topics we did: _____
   _____

2 Some new vocabulary I learned:

   Draw a picture in each box. Write the new words in the boxes under your pictures.

3 🎧 A song or story we listened to: _____

4 💬 Something we talked about: _____

5 🔍 Something we read about: _____

6 ✏️ Something we wrote about: _____

7 A game or activity I liked doing in class: _____

My Dossier

The activities in the dossier show what you can do in English.
You can put other work you did here, too.

What can you do in English?

	Contents	Date
1	A mythical creature	
2	A typical dish from my country	
3	A hobby or interest	
4	My school uniform design	
5	At the travel agency	
6		
7		

Great work!

A mythical creature

Invent a mythical creature or find one from a story or book that you like.
Draw a picture and write about your creature.

This mythical creature is called _____

What does it look like? _____
_____
_____

Where does it live? _____
_____
_____

What does it eat? _____
_____

More information: _____
_____

A typical dish from my country

Find a picture or draw a picture of a popular dish that people eat where you live.

What is the dish called? _____

What are the main ingredients? _____

_____

_____

_____

Do you eat this meal all the time or only on special occasions? If special occasions, which ones?

_____

What other food and drink do you have it with?

_____

_____

My hobby or interest

Do you have a special hobby? For example, do you play a sport or a musical instrument? Do you like collecting things? If you don't have a hobby, write about what you like doing in your free time.

My hobby/interest: _____
_____
_____
_____
_____

My school uniform design

Design a school uniform for children of the future. Describe it and say why they are going to wear these clothes.

At the travel agency

Work in pairs or groups of three. Write a dialog at the travel agency
(in a group of three, two of you are customers). Where do you want to go?
How much does it cost? How will you travel? Act your play out!

Customer: _____

_____

Travel agent: _____

_____

Customer: _____

_____

Travel agent: _____

_____

Customer: _____

_____

Travel agent: _____

_____

Customer: _____

_____

Thanks and Acknowledgments

Authors' thanks

Many thanks to everyone at Cambridge University Press and in particular to: Rosemary Bradley, for overseeing the whole project and successfully pulling it all together with good humor; Sarah McConnell, for her fine editorial skills and Karen Elliott for her enthusiasm and creative reworking of the Phonics sections.

We would also like to thank all our students and colleagues at Star English, El Palmar, Murcia, and especially Jim Kelly and Julie Woodman for their help, and suggestions at various stages of the project.

Dedications

For Carmen Navarro with love. Many thanks for all your hard work, help and support over the years – CN

To my Murcian family: Adolfo and Isabel, the Peinado sisters and their other halves for always treating me so well, Thanks for being there and for making my life in Murcia so much fun – MT

The Authors and Publishers would like to thank the following teachers for their help in reviewing the material and for the invaluable feedback they provided:

Carlos Astor Coll, Verónica Elizabeth Díaz Herrera, Irina Fedorova, Gabriela Finkelstein, Yesenia T. La Pierre Márquez, Violeta Gómez Tipula.

We would also like to thank all the teachers who allowed us to observe their classes and who gave up their invaluable time for interviews and focus groups.

The authors and publishers acknowledge the following sources of copyright material and are grateful for the permissions granted. While every effort has been made, it has not always been possible to identify the sources of all the material used or to trace all copyright holders. If any omissions are brought to our notice, we will be happy to include the appropriate acknowledgments on reprinting.

p. 6 (1): Shutterstock/© Petr Malyshev; p. 6 (2): Shutterstock/© wacpan; p. 6 (3): Shutterstock/© Tarzhanova; p. 6 (4 and 5): Shutterstock/© Igor Lateci; p. 6 (6): Shutterstock/© DVARG; p. 20 (1): Alamy/© colinspics; p. 20 (2): Shutterstock/© Minerva Studio; p. 20 (3): Alamy/© NASA Photography; p. 20 (4): Alamy/© Hongqi Zhang; p. 20 (B): Kennedy Space Center/© NASA; p. 24: © NASA; p. 38 (1): Shutterstock/© Ivonne Wierink; p. 38 (2): Shutterstock/© Fribus Ekaterina; p. 38 (3): Shutterstock/© Vlad Ageshin ; p. 38 (4): Shutterstock/© Elnur; p. 38 (5): Shutterstock/© NinaM ; p. 38 (6): Shutterstock/© Skylines; p. 38 (7): Shutterstock/© Alexander Dashewsky ; p. 38 (8): Shutterstock/© Matthew Benoit; p. 42: Shutterstock/© Edward Westmacott ; p. 50: Alamy/© Mark Conlin; p. 56 (1): Alamy/© Renegadephoto.net; p. 56 (2): Corbis/© Lwa-Stephen Welstead; p. 56 (3): Shutterstock/© Denis Radovanovic; p. 56 (4): Shutterstock/© Aletia; p. 56 (5): Shutterstock/© Kletr; p. 56 (B): Alamy/© GoodSportHD.com; p. 59 (T): Alamy/© Andrea Di Martino; p. 59 (B): Corbis/© Ludovic Maisant; p. 60: Alamy/© Keystone Pictures USA; p. 65 (1): Shutterstock/© Coprid; p. 65 (2): Shutterstock/© Fred Cardoso; p. 65 (3): Shutterstock/© Ma William Richardson; p. 65 (4): Shutterstock/© Forster Forest p. 66 (1): Shutterstock/© mrpuiii; p. 66 (2): Shutterstock/© Olga_Anourina; p. 66 (3): Shutterstock/© ajt; p. 66 (4): Shutterstock/© Venus Angel; p. 66 (5): Getty Images/E+/ yasinguneysu; p. 66 (6): Shutterstock/© windu; p. 70 (1): Thinkstock/istock/© Porechenskaya; p. 70 (2): Shutterstock/ Battrick; p. 70 (3): Alamy/© Radius Images; p. 70 (4): Shutterstock/© Andrey Nikulin; p. 70 (5): Alamy/© Mark Spowart.

The authors and publishers are grateful to the following illustrators:

Ilias Aravohitis c/o Beehive; Phil Burrows; R&C Burrows c/o Beehive; Moreno Chiacchiera, c/o Beehive; Christain Cornia c/o Advocate Art; FLP; Mark Duffin; Graham Kennedy; Mike Phillips; Mel Sharp, c/o Sylvie Poggio; Lisa Smith, c/o Sylvie Poggio; Jo Taylor, c/o Sylvie Poggio; Anthony Rule; Alan Row Gywneth Williamson

The publishers are grateful to the following contributors:

Stephen Bond: commissioned photography
Louise Edgeworth: picture research
Wild Apple Design Ltd: page design
Lon Chan: cover design
John Green and Tim Woolf, TEFL Audio: audio recordings
Songs written and produced by Robert Lee, Dib Dib Dub studios.
Rosalie Kerr: Flyers practice test
John Marshall Media, Inc. and Lisa Hutchins: audio recordin for the American English edition
hyphen S.A.: publishing management, American English edition